LIGHTPLANE
CONSTRUCTION
AND REPAIR

Introduction

Been moseying around airports lately? A bit bewildering, isn't it? The whine of jets . . . miles of paved runways . . . macadam parking lots . . . rows of brand-new hangars . . . gaily painted light (?) planes . . . gas trucks . . . uniformed attendants . . . brightly lit shops . . . almost like a military reservation. Nary an *old* plane in sight, seems like!

Look a little further—over on the far side of the field. One of these proud old ladies might be just the one you've been looking for. Sure, she may be a bit tattered, but all it takes to transform her is a loving hand . . . and a willingness to work.

The authors of this book hope to guide your loving hand by showing you the way.

LIGHTPLANE CONSTRUCTION AND REPAIR

by Al Snyder and William A. Welch

Contents

1. What You Should Know Before Starting

The most crucial part of aircraft repair or construction is the part *before* you cut a single piece of stock. Detailed planning goes a long way toward a smooth, enjoyable project. From a complete list of the operations to be performed you can determine what equipment will be needed, what regulations apply, and what facilities you must have. FAA requires inspections and records that are easy to provide —if planned in advance.

Work is governed by Federal Aviation Regulations (FAR) published and administered by the Federal Aviation Agency (FAA), entirely to ensure public safety. Standards of safety apply to both design and workmanship.

You'll find a visit to your local FAA District Office will be most enlightening and helpful. With a few exceptions the maintenance inspectors will be very interested, helpful and informative about your project whether it's a repair of a Type-Certificated aircraft or an Amateur built from a set of plans. Just remember most of these men were mechanics for many years before they joined the FAA. So they have a wealth of experience which you can draw on and it's for free. All you have to do is ask for it. They will give you a run-down on the regulations that apply to your situation and the various procedures you'll have to follow to keep within the law as they must enforce it.

The FAA issues many pamphlets, booklets, Advisory Circulars, etc. which you can obtain either from FAA directly or through the Superintendent of Documents, U.S. Government Printing Office, Washington, D.C. 20402. (Many are free.) One you *should* order is the bible of repair and construction: FAA AC no. 43.13-1, *Acceptable Methods, Techniques, and Practices—Aircraft Inspection and Repair*. It really goes into detail in a readable way and is based on many, many years of experience throughout the industry.

Protection is afforded the public against irresponsible persons, but the individual is free to accept his own risks provided he doesn't endanger anyone else. Aircraft are classified in two categories for safety regulations, those built under Approved Type Certificates, and those not certificated. Only one classification is open to the amateur for non-certificated aircraft. That is the Experimental, Amateur-Built class, which is subject to very strict limitations. Airplanes for unrestricted use must comply with Approved Type Certificates. The best way to make sure of your position is to consult the FAA District Office as soon as you have prepared an outline of the work you propose to do. Check especially these points:

- What parts of the work you may legally perform yourself
- What inspections are required
- Who will inspect the work
- Basis of design approval
- If design is not approved, what flight restrictions will be applied
- Records required for purchased materials

Because every case is different, the following chapters can offer only a general guide to the regulations, and direct contact with the FAA is usually necessary. Besides the FAA there are two other "friends" you should cultivate. One is your local airport operator. It's on his field where you'll keep your newly acquired mistress and you may decide to rent a hangar to work on your project 'til she's ready to take wing. He's also a source of information on all things airlike so make friends early.

The other is that stalwart fellow with a tool box as a third arm— the A&P Mechanic. Since you'll require his services quite frequently, you'd better find a kindly soul with patience and a little time to spend with you in the evening or on a weekend. It will help the bonds of friendship if you mention that you're willing to pay for his services—within reason of course. It wouldn't hurt to get a few recommendations from the local FAA boys while you're talking with them. They're in a position to know. Once you find the good guy, heed his advice and ask him all the questions you can think of. He'll be flattered and you'll get an education.

By definition, repairing is restoring something to a former state, and that's just what aircraft repair is. There is one exception. Replacement with a different, but equally suitable, part is legal. This may take considerable proving, however.

Older aircraft can be a special problem, if the original manufacturer is out of business. Necessary information can be obtained from FAA records, but this may be slow and costly because these are only copies, not reproducible masters. If the Type Certificate is owned by a currently active person or firm, an inquiry to the FAA District Office will turn up the address.

Repairs are governed by Part 43 of the Federal Aviation Regulations. Repairs on certificated aircraft must be performed by certificated mechanics, or *under their supervision*. Complete records must be kept, in the aircraft log book for minor repairs, and in Form ACA-337 for major repairs or alterations.

Approved designs for repairs can be found in FAA AC 43.13-1 and -2, in the manufacturer's Service Manual, or sometimes by contacting the manufacturer directly. If the situation is not covered by any of these ready-made repair designs, then specific engineering approval must be obtained for your own design. The applicant must provide engineering data to prove the proposed design actually meets safety requirements. When a substantial amount of engineering effort is required, the process can usually be speeded up by retaining a Designated Engineering Representative to prepare the material. FAA offices can furnish a list of consulting DERs.

Maintenance, of course, means keeping the equipment in airworthy condition so that repairs are not needed. FAR 43 specifies the preventive maintenance operations which may be performed by a licensed pilot on aircraft he owns or operates. For all other maintenance, the supervision and approval of a licensed mechanic are required. All maintenance is to be recorded in a permanent record, usually the logbook, with the signature of the person responsible for it.

Each aircraft has its own peculiar needs in addition to the obvious things that all planes require. The manufacturer's maintenance manual should be used to make certain these needs are met.

FAA issues Airworthiness Directives, or ADs, when the need arises for a *mandatory* change in any certificated aircraft to maintain it in a safe condition, or to correct a potentially dangerous condition. If the situation is urgent, all registered owners of the type are contacted immediately. Otherwise, each AD includes a date or total service time considered safe before the change must be incorporated.

A *Summary* of all ADs is published, and copies may be obtained from the FAA Washington office. Occasionally an AD is very costly because of extensive dismantling or rework. When buying an older model plane, you should check the paperwork (logs and attached Forms 337 for airplane and engine) to be sure the necessary modifications have been done. The signature and certificate number of a licensed mechanic are required in such entries. Here's where your A&P friend can be of great help. Have him check over the papers and the aircraft before you buy and let him give you his opinion on how much it will cost to get the ship into airworthy condition. The few bucks you pay him may save you many hundreds, even thousands of dollars. It may be that the seller is trying to sell you a dog but more likely he doesn't really know the condition of his own ship. No use your buying someone else's problems unless you know them and feel it's worth it.

Aside from the ADs, maintenance generally consists of lubrication, cleaning, refinishing, replacement of worn parts, adjustment, and other such minor (but very important) operations necessary to keep the aircraft in good condition. If you fly, offer airplanes for sale, or offer to sell rides in airplanes, the law compels you to respect the safety of other persons and their property. You are not forbidden personal risk, as long as it does not affect others. That is the whole basis for the regulations which govern modification and construction of airplanes.

To be certificated for general use, an aircraft must conform to an Approved Type Design, which is covered by an Approved Type Certificate, and possibly by one or more Supplemental Type Certificates. Aircraft which are not certificated for general use are limited to specified purposes, and usually restricted to certain areas and airports. Airplanes in the experimental, amateur-built category may be given a go-anywhere approval after accumulating a certain number of hours, but will not be allowed to carry persons or cargo for hire.

If you plan to construct an airplane or modify one, you must decide whether you wish to have completely unrestricted use of the ship or not. Unless you are willing to accept the experimental restrictions, your choice of aircraft is limited to those for which type approval has been established. A list of Supplemental Type Certificates and Approved Replacement Parts is available from the FAA Washington office. This includes all STCs for which parts or data can be purchased. If there is any doubt concerning plans or parts you may wish to use, an inquiry to the nearest FAA District Office will determine if approval has been granted.

When building or modifying to approved designs, you need to remember that someone authorized for the purpose must inspect the work to verify that it does conform to the design. Definite appointments with the inspector should be made in advance to provide him sufficient opportunity to see the work before it is covered up.

The Experimental, Amateur-Built category offers a lot more freedom in exchange for the operating limitations. You may choose your design freely, but watch out for kits. Standard parts such as engines, wheels, instruments, and so on may be purchased within the intent of the regulations. However, FAA has found it necessary to issue a warning on kits—Advisory Circular No. 20-28, dated 8-7-64. Aircraft built from kits may not be eligible for the Amateur-Built category. The status of any kit can be checked with the District Office.

Sets of plans for airplanes can be purchased from a number of sources, and several of them are advertised in national aviation periodicals. Some of these plans are well known and have been used by many builders with excellent results. There is at least one organization* of national scope which specializes in amateur airplane-building activities. The experiences of such a group should be considered by any amateur builder in selecting the design for his projects. You probably have a local chapter in your area. Stop in at one of the regular meetings, you'll spend a most enjoyable evening . . . with fellow amateurs.

Numbered forms have become a part of our technical existence and aviation is no exception. Every ship that is meant to fly has at least a Registration Certificate and an Airworthiness Certificate. Then there is a log book for the aircraft and another for the engine. You must also show evidence of the status of weight and balance, an equipment list (radio, lights, etc.) and the Operation and Limitations record for the particular make and model (speed ranges for gear, flaps, never exceed; maximum gross weight, maximum rpm of engine with oil temperature and pressure ranges, etc.).

On older models you have a whole wad of Form ACA 337s, namely the Repair and Alteration records of the aircraft and engine. If you recover the wings, your mechanic will fill out the 337

---

*Experimental Aircraft Association, Hales Corners, Wisconsin.

and have another mechanic with an IA rating (Inspection Authorization) also sign the 337 to release it for flight. The IA is empowered within certain limits to act for the FAA. It may be that your A&P has this rating so he can sign as the A&P and also as the IA. Incidentally, the FAA will supply all of these forms free of charge on request. If you're planning to build under the experimental or amateur category, you'll have to apply for the registration numbers . . . this will cost a few dollars, but the forms are for free.

Weight and Balance

Aircraft weight and balance control and records aren't really difficult. Some people just make it sound complicated. Important it is, but difficult it is not. The pilot's ability to control the airplane is drastically affected by the center of gravity (CG) position.

Let's begin with a definition. Center of gravity means an imaginary point about which a complete body is balanced. In the seesaw, the combined weight of the board and riders is balanced at the pivot. If it weren't, one end would go down till it hit the ground. Thus the pivot is also the CG of the seesaw.

You instinctively know that a small weight located far from the pivot can balance a heavy weight close to it. In order to make use of this relationship we must have a measure. If we multiply the weight by the distance from the pivot, the product is exactly proportional to the ability of one weight to balance another. This product is called the "moment" of the weight about a pivot. Actually, the moment can be taken about any point, and need not refer to any physical feature such as a pivot.

The fuss and bother with airplane weight and balance is all about the CG location, simply because there is only a limited range of CG positions in which successful flight is at all likely or even possible. A real tame airplane can become violently unstable with a CG position outside the suitable range, or it can lack the necessary control effectiveness to execute the most essential maneuver.

To determine where the airplane CG is, we can add up the moments of all the weights in it about some arbitrary point. Then, naturally, if we divide this total moment by the total weight, the result is the distance from our reference point to the airplane CG. It's really just that simple. Anything more about weight and balance is merely building some detail on top of that, or prescribing a recipe to be followed step by step.

In reality, there are three versions of the CG problem you may have to solve. These are:

1. *Where is the CG, given all the weights and their locations?*
2. *Given this airplane, and this CG position limit, how much weight can be loaded in what position?*
3. *Given this airplane, what are the weight and CG position?*

The first of these is handled most conveniently by taking the total empty weight of the airplane as one item located at the CG of the total. Usually, this is available from the manufacturer. On an amateur-built aircraft or newly repaired one, it may be necessary to measure the information. Unusable fuel in the tanks, and fluids trapped in lines are always included in the empty weight. Each item of disposable load is treated separately, as shown below, including each seat, each tank, and each baggage position. The tabular form is convenient, and reduces errors.

Item	*Weight*	*Station*	*Moment*
empty weight	800	100	80,000
pilot	150	120	18,000
passenger	150	120	18,000
baggage	50	150	7,500
fuel	180	90	16,200
oil	10	10	100
gross weight	1340	104.3	139,800

The reference or datum point is often chosen ahead of the airplane nose, so that all numbers in the computation are positive. Some airplanes have other reference stations, such as the leading edge of the wing or the firewall. The only difference in the arithmetic is that stations forward of the reference are considered negative, and you have to keep track of the positive and negative signs. That's a little easier if you use a separate column for each, and subtotal them.

The second problem, how much load can be placed in what position, is readily solved by means of two simultaneous equations. Don't let that frighten you. It's just a formal name for a very simple bit of logic. Here's how it works. Suppose we know the maximum gross weight allowed, and the most rearward CG limit.

Now assume we must load the airplane to maximum gross weight without exceeding the rearward limit. Since the empty weight is known, the maximum load is found by simple subtraction. If the fuel load is known, like full tanks, then we have just a certain weight allowance left for, say, the passenger seat and baggage. If we call the seat load A, and the baggage load B, we know that A plus B must be equal to some number, the remaining weight allowance. Writing this as an equation, we get:

$$A + B = W$$

Now we also know the CG position for the gross weight, or to put it another way, we know the *moment* of the gross weight. Besides that we know the stations of the two loads to be added. Calling the stations respectively x and y, the last statements can be written as another equation where M is the gross-weight moment, less the empty-weight moment:

$$Ax + By = M$$

By multiplying the first equation with y, then subtracting it from the second equation, a new one is formed with no B in it. This we can solve for A, which gives:

(equation 1)

$$A = \frac{M - Wy}{x - y}$$

To find B now, just take

(equation 2)

$$B = W - A$$

That's all there is to it. Just use equations 1 and 2, remembering that A and x are the weight and station that go together for one load, B and y for the other load, and M is the gross-weight moment minus the empty-weight moment. For an aft load condition this gives the maximum load in the more aft position B which will not violate the rearward limit. If the gross weight moment you use is that for the most forward CG position, the load at A is the maximum that will not violate the *forward* limit.

Ready for the third problem? This one is no harder than the other two, but there is more to do. Weighing the airplane must be done with extreme care to get accurate results, because the whole operation is very sensitive to small errors. First, the airplane must be leveled. Be careful to understand clearly what this means. All weight and balance computations are based on *horizontal* moment arms or stations. Therefore, the reference line parallel to these dimensions is what must be leveled. This may well *not* be the way the airplane sets on its landing gear, and may require blocking up one end or the other. Airplanes are required by FAA to be equipped with levelling reference points, and these are described in the manufacturer's handbooks. A difference of only two degrees can introduce a serious error. For example, if a wheel is 30 inches below the reference station mark on the airplane, two degrees gives an error of about one inch in the station of the wheel. For this reason, measurements involving points at different heights on the airplane should be made with plumb lines.

The most accurate level you can readily obtain for longer reaches is a garden hose, or even several of them coupled together, filled with water (carefully—no bubbles). Especially with the transparent type, you can easily measure equal heights to one hundredth of an inch, a hundred feet apart. Surveying instruments don't usually do any better. The second most accurate is the longest plumb line you can hang across the marks on the airplane. A carpenter's or mason's level should only be used with grave reservations as a last resort.

Weighing the Airplane

The next most important part of the setup is to make sure the forces acting on your scales are indeed vertical forces. If the scale platform is loaded horizontally, it is likely to bind and give completely false readings. Any landing gear in which the wheel moves laterally, as the spring type gear, can cause this type of difficulty. It can be avoided by careful positioning, lubrication under the wheel, or metal or wood plates with rollers under the wheel to reduce lateral friction.

Although it is theoretically possible to weigh the airplane one wheel at a time, it isn't practical because the exact positioning just doesn't get reproduced from one wheel to the next. Results are not accurate. So, have scales under all wheels at once.

Since you will probably modify the chocks and blocks after getting the airplane onto the scales, make sure these bits and pieces are kept on the scales after you take the airplane off. They are the tare weights you have to deduct from the scale readings to get the airplane weight.

Once everything is steady on the scales, the airplane is level, and you're ready to take your readings, shake the airplane (gently) in pitch and roll to make sure all scales are free; then proceed. Again disturb the ship a little and take a second set of readings; then a third. They will differ some. If they differ a lot, recheck the whole setup, because something is basically wrong with it. Close readings may be averaged for best results.

Once the readings are corrected for tare, and you have the measured weight at each wheel, simple addition, of course, gives the airplane weight. The CG location takes a little more arithmetic. It must lie between the wheels, of course, so we need only one number, the distance from one wheel or pair of wheels.

The most convenient reference for this is one of the wheel stations, since the load at that station then has no moment, and only one moment is needed. Taking moments about the nose wheel station, for example, the moment of the total load on the main wheels must be identical to the moment of the whole airplane. Therefore, we simply multiply the total main wheel load by the distance from nose to main wheels, and divide the product by the weight of the whole airplane. The result is the distance from nose wheel to CG. This is converted to airplane station, or distance from the reference point, by simply adding it to the nose wheel station.

Remember, the weight you measure should be the empty weight of the airplane, so tanks should be drained first. Also, any loose equipment not considered part of the airplane should be removed before weighing. Anything built in or permanently fixed to the ship is included in the weighing.

A very simple chart is often used to keep track of the weight and balance, and it appears in many pilot's manuals. This is merely a chart showing moment as a function of weight. The moment for any one load item is just a straight line from the origin, and the limiting CG positions can be shown as boundary lines, usually straight, indicating the total airplane moment for each gross weight.

2. Dismantling the Aircraft

As a general rule, nobody has any trouble getting anything *apart*. It's when you try to put the whole works back *together* again that you start to realize parts are missing, this should have been put together before that, etc.

So let's talk about *how* to take something apart. A good set of tools is really helpful, in fact you'll find the job most difficult without them. Most of the engineers who design these flying machines never seem to get around to working on them. Look good on paper, but . . . well, that's past history. You'll just have to make do, but the tools are a MUST.

First, if the wings are to be removed, drain the gas. It may surprise you to know that a full tank of gas weighs more than the wing. Figure it out. A panel weighs from 60 to 100 pounds on the average strut-braced, fabric-covered light plane. The tanks run from 12.5 to 25 gallons—that's 75 to 150 pounds. So get the gas out first.

Start right now to put hardware back in place, finger-tight, as you go along. The gas plug would be one of the first items. Now remove all the fairing which needs to be removed for the job you intend doing. Get a pail or bucket for the loose parts. Write location of parts and pairing of wires on masking tape and stick on everything as you go along. It'll take the mystery out of such comments as, "Now let's see—where does this go?" With the fairing removed, look over the butt of the wing. Wiring can be unclipped and marked. Use masking tape on each wire, then mark with 1-1, 2-2, etc.

Then the gas line. Hose clamps usually require only a screwdriver or pliers. If it is a tube fitting, apply the wrench carefully. Watch the tubing on both sides of the fitting. If both turn, stop. Get a wrench on the male fitting also. Once you turn or break the two fittings, the tubing will usually remain stationary. If not, you may have to use pliers directly on the tubing. This is not recommended, however, and you'll have to be very careful. If the tubing is damaged by twisting, or gouged by teeth marks, you'll have to replace that part. A bit of tape on the nose of the pliers will help.

With drift pin and hammer the front strut bolt is easily removed. One man must hold the strut so that the clevis bolt won't be bent in the process of removal.

Next the control cables to the flaps and ailerons. Look over the parts manual first, if you have one. It will tell you where the turn-buckles are. It's always the least amount of work to remove nuts and bolts rather than unsafety the turnbuckles. You won't have to re-rig the cables when you put everything back together again.

If the wings are to be re-covered, just tear the fabric to get at the cable fittings. The Piper Tri-Pacer has three such attachments (one for flap and two for aileron) just aft of the rear spar on the inboard side. The Stinson, on the other hand, can best be unhooked from inside the cabin. Remove a turnbuckle and pulley behind the rear seat and slip a bolt on the cross-over cable for the aileron. Slip a bolt and pulley at center and overhead for the flap. Pull cables from fuselage, coil and tape. On the Cessna 140, it's best to remove the aileron control arm from the idler, and then the idler from its bracket. It will then hang from the wing by the two cables. Slip the bolts attaching the cables to the idler. Replace all the bolts, nuts, washers and bushings in the proper order. If the idler is to be left out of the wing, mark it—it's too easy to be confused with the other hand. Tie a cord to each cable, then pull through the wing. Gently, gently—or you may tear the ribs. Other types have similar arrangements. A little forethought will save extra expense and hours of added work.

Now loop the cables over the aft fuselage so they won't drag on the ground, or push them into the fuselage. (Flaps on the Cessna 140 are bolted to a torque tube. Remember to remove this bolt, or you'll bend something when trying to remove the wing.)

You can remove the ailerons and flaps at this point, or wait until you have them on a bench. Now all you have to remove are the two butt bolts, two wing-strut bolts and fuselage-to-strut bolts. First remove all the nuts. Then get a couple of friends to hold the wing while you remove the bolts. Make sure the wing is held in its original position until the butt bolts are removed; you might crack a fitting at the butt of the wing otherwise. Unless a wing is going to be put back in a short time, it's best to remove and store the struts in a safe place. Most struts must be removed before the wing so you won't bend the fittings at either end.

Don't lay the wing down just anywhere. If you happen to be outside and the wind is up a bit, you just might find yourself chasing that wing right to the junkpile! Make sure it's secure, then it's easier to keep your cool, Dad. It's a good idea to make a few notes and sketches as you go along. Keep in mind that it may be months before you put the ship back together again.

Removing the tail feathers may be almost as much of a job as the wings. The hardware is more difficult to get at and sometimes it takes a lot of patience. Again, look over the parts manual if you have one. If you don't, then look over the attachments after you get the

It helps to have a lot of help but why the two guys at the light end?
After removing the butt bolts the wing drops down easily.

fairings off. On some ships the rudder and fin are independently
mounted so that removing one doesn't mean having to remove the
other. Once you have it apart, put the hardware back finger-tight—
use cord or safety wire on the cables so you won't have to crawl
back in the fuselage to retrieve them.

Now that you have things all apart, it's a good time to inspect
all the systems: controls, electrical, vacuum, radio, lights. Clean out
the fuselage, remove rust and corrosion, lubricate pulleys and bearings, protect cables. Chromate the inside as the manufacturer never
did. It's much easier now than later and can be done more completely and with less effort. Now is a good time, too, to check over
all the hardware. Make a list, then order with the rest of the parts
you'll need.

Many low-wing ships have the gear attached to the wings and
they, in turn, attach to the fuselage. If you have this type, you will
have to make a cradle and dolly (if you are going to want to move
the ship around). The position of the cradle will also depend on

whether or not the engine is to be removed. The engine will weigh almost as much as the fuselage, so make a long cradle or use an individual stand at the tail. The important consideration in making the cradle is "where will it bear on the fuselage?" Consider whether repairs would mean moving the fuselage from the cradle. In such a case, maybe a dolly attached to the wing-attach points would allow more flexibility, both in repair and painting. With a few pieces of pipe, a set of axles and wheels from a crack-up, and a few hours' labor you will have a flexible setup.

At some point you'll have to remove an engine, either because it's tired or you've got a slightly retracted nose wheel which wasn't designed to be, or for other reasons. At any rate, let's get the cowling off first so we can see what we've mistakenly done to our bird. This done, unspin the spinner and cut the safety wire on the prop.

By the way, did you check the switch—is it off? Just one swipe with that big razor will keep you clean for months! You might even run the carburetor dry by turning the gas off till it quits. You'll find it a safe rule to *always* turn the prop backwards or clockwise. The impulse won't work nor will the timing. It just won't run or even kick.

So after you've removed the safety wire and bolts use a marking pencil to mark the position of all spinner parts and prop to the hub. Now turn the prop to a horizontal position, grasp firmly and work back and forth from one blade to the other. Remember, the prop weighs 30 to 50 pounds if it's metal. Once it comes loose, you've got to be prepared to handle the weight without dropping it. Don't use anything to pry the prop off. You'll most likely only succeed in denting or scoring the hub of both the shaft and the prop. This could lead to a failure of one or both at a most inconvenient time— like 50 feet over the wrong end of the runway. Just be patient, and maybe use a little penetrating oil—even let it set overnight, then it'll almost fall off. Once off, lay the prop down flat on some rags or wood blocks. Standing it up on edge may take less room but it is inviting damage through tipping over and thus denting or nicking the edges. Keep in mind that it's your GO producer,

Removing the engine isn't hard work until the very last. But make sure that everything is disconnected. Carburetor gas line, generator, starter, mag, head temp, etc.; wires and leads, carb heater and throttle and mixture controls; hoses of all kinds, and, in some cases, the exhaust manifolds and/or intake manifolds. Also drain the oil or you'll have it all over the place. Even the plugs and leads may be affected, just anything that might interfere with the removal. Also support the tail with a sawhorse or something. At this point it might be advisable to make a few notes so as to avoid extra work in the installation, and so that you can have them to jog your memory later.

The last thing would be the engine mount bolts—but only when you've got enough help or a good hoist. Most engines have a lifting ring which is usually at the balance point. If not, then use an old control cable . . . doubled. Most of the smaller engines weigh 200 to 300 pounds so you'll need three or four strong friends. Think ahead—where are you going to put the engine? If it's on the floor, then set it on a couple of wooden blocks, usually on its back so as not to bend the carburetor mounting studs or the carburetor. Once it's off, you'd better collect all the parts in one place. There are many special bits of hardware which are hard to come by when you need them. With the engine out, you will be free to work the forward part of your machine with much more ease.

Now, with the craft apart, you'll be ordering the parts you will need to make the necessary repairs. Don't forget the hardware. Dig it out and look it over. If it's not up to standard, get new. There are less than $20 worth of nuts, bolts, and screws in most lightplanes, yet about 50% of the time to put the thing together is spent in hunting for hardware!

Hauling—from and to—the airport, can cause as much or sometimes more damage than was done in the first place. But the moving need not be painful to either your pocketbook or the aircraft. You can, at little cost, rent a van or stake-bodied truck at so much a day plus mileage. Another way is with a set of car roof-racks for the wings and some sort of bumper hitch to secure the tail. In any case, you'll need lots of rope, blankets or cardboard, old tires or tubes, anything that is soft and that will keep the metal surface or fabric from being chafed.

Usually the roof-rack idea is the best for wings and control surfaces. Attach about six or eight feet of 2 x 4 on either side of the racks running fore and aft. Secure to the racks with wire or, better yet, bolts. By positioning the racks you can lay the first wing in broad contact with the 2 x 4s (cushioned with rags or cardboard, of course), bottom side down, with butt or inboard end of the wing forward. Lay a couple of blankets at either end so that the other wing can be laid top side down. This will put both top sides together. If there are extended vents on the tanks which are difficult to remove, the top side curvature of the wings will usually be enough to keep them from hitting the other surface.

Rope both surfaces together, from one side of each rack over the wings to the other side. Pull firmly but not so tightly as to bend something. That's what we're trying to avoid. Now tie the spar fitting at the butt together, then cross-tie to the front bumper. Use rope not wire, or you'll score the bolt holes. Do the same at the wing tips but remember that the ribs are very thin metal and may tear easily. Usually the tip ends of the wings are light so you need not tie down at the tips at all. Ailerons and flaps, if not installed on the wings, can be wrapped in blankets and lashed to the top of the two wings. Since the wings are the lightest part of your load, the roof-rack idea will give them an easier ride and less jostling around than any other method. Trucks, except for the very light ones, have heavy springs to take heavy loads. The result is a rough ride for a light load.

There are several ways you can haul the fuselage, depending on the position of the gear and/or whether the gear is part of the wings. If the gear is rollable, then either the tail wheel spring or skid (tri-gear) may be attached to the rear bumper. If you can't adapt a regular trailer hitch, then make one of your own. Your local hardware store sells strap steel which you can bend to hook around your bumper. Take two pieces, make a hook in each, then form one top and the other bottom around the curve of the bumper. Leave enough to form a leg on each with space between for a bolt to draw up tight. This will clamp onto the bumper and leave enough to which the tail may be attached.

With a tri-gear, either remove the nose wheel and strut or remove the air pressure in the strut and tie in the compressed position. Better check the brakes for drag and the wheel bearings for grease. Most aircraft wheels never turn for long periods and may get hot and even burn out. So a little checking will help avoid extra problems.

It would be a good idea also to check with the State Police of all states you will be passing through so as to avoid unnecessary violations of regulations for hauling. Usually they require a red flag about 18" square, and lights if you're hauling at night. If the load is over a certain length or width, you can get a permit for a few bucks and observe special rules of the road.

Where the gear isn't roadable, a boat trailer or a U-Haul-It type can be rented from your local gas station. It's built for light loads and will do just fine for your fuselage. Here again, use old tires, blankets, tubes, wooden forms, anything which will support the structure and not damage it more than it is. Lash down all around, hook up and be gone. It's natural not to be as fussy before the repairs are made but it would be a downright shame to get all set up to put the little lady back together again, only to find that she's been mussed up getting back to the airport. Of course, that trip will take more of the same care we've talked about before—only this time with pride.

What Parts, Components and Materials to Use

Whether you are repairing a damaged ship, doing routine maintenance, or building from a set of plans . . . you've got a parts problem. If it is a current model, or even an older model that the manufacturer still makes parts for, you'll find it a bit easier except that you may have to wait for weeks after you place your order. Usually the manufacturer's dealer and distributor organization will be of great help. They will have a parts manual which gives a pictorial view of each part with referenced numbers to the parts list. All you need is the model, year of manufacture, and the aircraft's serial number. You will find a manufacturer's registration plate with all this information somewhere on the fuselage frame. (Of course, this info is also in the aircraft's log books.)

When you get the ordered parts, they will be identified by part numbers on the packing slip and either on the part itself or, in the case of small parts, on an envelope with the parts in it. Keep all this information so you can prove that the parts are genuine. Standard hardware will have self-identification—for example, markings on the head of the bolt. This will satisfy your mechanic and the FAA as to parts certification.

Some older or modified aircraft are orphans. They present a real problem as to where to get parts. If the type and model were produced in some quantity you will find many companies specializing in the manufacture and sale of their parts. *Trade-A-Plane* is an excellent source of where to buy such parts as are other aviation publications such as *Air Progress, Flying, AOPA Pilot,* etc. Not only the display ads, but also the classified, should be checked for possible leads. If you cannot find what you want, try putting an ad in the classified columns yourself. Some of the most hard-to-get parts for older aircraft have been found in just this way. You might also make a tour of local airports, especially the older ones. Ask around. Leave your name. It's surprising what can sometimes be turned up this way.

Used parts dealers are another widely used source. These used parts come from wrecks or the cannibalizing of complete ships. There are used parts dealers all over the country. Some advertise nationally, others only locally; some never advertise—they're just known. Usually you'll find that most of these dealers will stand back of what they sell, or will at least tell you what to expect and let you decide for yourself whether or not you can use the part.

But the very nature of the used parts business says, "Buyer Beware!" It will pay you to look carefully before you buy. Get an A&P mechanic to look over the parts if a lot of money is involved and you are not sure of the dealer's integrity. Try to get a written guarantee of the part's condition and whether the dealer will give you your money back if you are not satisfied. If he won't—try somewhere else first.

What if the parts aren't obtainable? Then make 'em! If the old part can give you enough information, all you'll have to do is get the right materials and fabricate the part, or have someone that knows how do it for you. Granted it will take some doing, but isn't that part of the fun? Just make sure to keep the old part around to prove the replacement is equal to, or better than, the old one.

As a last resort, you can contact either the manufacturer or current Type Certificate holder for a drawing or drawings of the parts. If they are not available, then ask for written permission to release the drawings from the FAA files. You won't get the original drawings, of course, but they will be released to an approved bonded copying firm who will make copies from the originals for you. Naturally, this all costs money (although it's not as expensive as you might think) and it will take time.

Usually when a couple of guys get talking about building an airplane, somebody suggests taking a wing from this one, a tail from another, etc., until you've got a flying machine. That's about all it ever amounts to, though—talk! Oh, sure, there have been hybrids, but they're very rare and usually the builder wishes he'd started from scratch because the ship never performs as well as he'd thought it would. At best, such an airplane is a vast series of compromises. There are many notable examples, with very few getting through the prototype stage. Occasionally, though, you can adapt parts or components which were designed for universal use—wheels, brakes, tires, wires, cable, hardware, instruments, engines, gear legs, lights and the like.

Major body parts or components—such as wings, tail surfaces, flaps, fuselages, ailerons—were designed to meet specific loads and flight conditions which are never quite the same with another design. Either they are too weak for one condition or too strong and heavy for others. At any rate, you'd find it would require the services of a qualified aeronautical engineer to make an analysis to determine if such parts could be used safely and to advantage. The cost to have an engineer do this will bring you off Cloud Nine in a hurry. In fact, you could take the same amount of cash to the same engineer and come up with a design which would be more worth the effort. Take some advice: Just have fun *talking* about it!

Material selection is one of the more difficult things for the amateur mechanic or builder to appreciate, because the right answer *seems* obvious, and it really isn't. Whether you are repairing or replacing an existing part, or making a brand-new one, it is often necessary to find an acceptable substitute for the original material.

The first thought most of us have is that anything stronger will do. On the surface, it seems logical. Actually, it's true only sometimes. If the material is stronger *but not stiffer,* the substitution is okay. Unfortunately, a greater stiffness often goes along with higher strength.

The reason stiffness is so important is that it controls the distribution of loads among the members of a structure. Most aircraft structures are redundant to some extent. This means they have more than the minimum possible number of members; or another way to put it is that there are at least two load paths. Given a choice, the loads will head for the stiffest path.

Two of the most common aircraft materials provide the classic example of the danger in careless selection: cold-rolled plain carbon steel and 2024-T4 aluminum alloy. The steel has almost the same breaking strength as the aluminum alloy, slightly higher. However, it has about three times the stiffness. If you have a structure of aluminum alloy members and put in one steel piece, the load will concentrate in the steel member. It will actually break with a *smaller* load on the structure than the 2024 piece. The same result will occur if the part is made stronger by using a material of lower strength and making it thicker. Again, even if the original breaking load of the individual part is reproduced, the added thickness will make it stiffer, and it will be forced to carry more than its share of the total load on a structure.

Lower stiffness is also to be avoided because that throws load to other members, and may well cause them to fail prematurely.

In general, to a close enough approximation, all the aluminum alloys have the same stiffness (elastic modulus), another applies to all steels, another to brasses, and another to copper. The plastics vary widely, even within a given type of material, since the properties depend upon the fabricating processes and any reinforcements such as glass fiber cloth or mat. While the elastic modulus is the same for all metals of a given family, the strengths may vary over an extremely wide range. The strongest steel available in commercial product form has about *ten times* the strength of the weakest.

There are two ways the strengths of metals are improved, heat treating and cold working. Some alloys will respond to one of these methods, others to both. The alloying elements are usually chosen to impart some other qualities, such as corrosion resistance, machinability, weldability, impact resistance, or magnetic properties.

Surface hardness can be increased by several treatments in steels, such as carburizing (case-hardening) and nitriding. However, these processes are of little interest for airframe parts. They are extensively used in engine and power transmission components. Comparable treatments are also available for aluminum alloys. Hard chrome plating has been used in place of hardening treatments. However, it should *never* be applied to aircraft parts without complete fatigue-life testing, because it causes a definite loss of fatigue strength. This disadvantage is overbalanced by a desirable effect in some applications, such as cylinder barrel liners for engines. Being brittle, the chrome develops a network of cracks, which are terrible for strength, but they act as reservoirs for lubricants. Hard chrome plating is therefore approved for some engines.

Generally, only a few of the hundreds of existing metals and plastics need be considered for building and repairing lightplanes. The following list covers the most commonly specified materials for airframe structural parts and includes at least one of each type of alloy needed.

Aluminum alloys

5052-O	dead soft	For general non-structural use,
-H32	quarter hard	weldable, strain-hardening type.
-H38	full hard	Cowl, fairings, tip caps, etc.
2024-O	dead soft	General structural alloy—may
-T3	heat treated and cold worked	be used in Alclad form for corrosion resistance.
-T4	heat treated	

Steels

SAE 4130 normalized		General structural steel in tube, bar, sheet.
AISI Type 302 annealed hard		General purpose corrosion-resistant steel. Strain-hardening type, may be welded, formed, machined.

Other metals are usually purchased only in the form of manufactured products, such as porous bronze (self-lubricating) bushings, gears, and other comparatively standard components. Therefore, no attempt is made here to give details.

Metal stock is often used in the annealed form to facilitate forming or manufacturing. No annealed material should ever be permitted in the airplane. At the very least, strain-hardening due to forming should be retained in the final part. The heat treatable aluminum alloys and normalizing steels should be fully heat treated or normalized before use in the airplane. Aluminum alloys can be heat treated only by properly equipped shops which specialize in such operations. 4130 steel can be normalized satisfactorily by heating cherry-red with a torch, and permitting the metal to air cool. If heat treatment other than normalizing is required on steel, it should be done by a specialty shop.

When structural aluminum alloy (2024) parts are made from soft-temper material and heat treated, they usually require some straightening or smoothing *after* heat treatment. At room temperature, 2024 remains workable about a half hour after it is quenched (the final step in heat treatment). Longer than that after quench, so little ductility remains that even moderate forming will crack the part. If the half hour isn't enough to get parts back to your own shop, don't give up. You can pack the material in dry ice and keep it in workable condition as long as overnight if necessary. The longer it is held, the less time there is to work on it once it warms up, however.

The only other common metal that deserves attention here is the aluminum alloy rivet. Only one type of rivet makes sense, unless something else is specifically called out on the drawings. That one is the "type AD" 2117-T4 rivet, which can be cold-driven as received from the mill. Rivets of other alloys must be kept at low temperatures after quenching, until driven.

Reinforced plastic materials are discussed in Chapter 7 as part of the construction technique because the material itself only develops its inherent properties as a result of the construction.

4. Covering with Fabrics and Forming Plexiglas

Fabric for the covering of aircraft is as old as aviation itself and probably will be used for many years to come. It still offers a cheap and easy way to cover the many surfaces of an aircraft. Some lightplane manufacturers and most amateur builders still find it suits their designs best. Of course there have been many changes since the early days. Not in basic application but in the material itself.

Twenty years ago the only materials were cotton and linen. Today, however, there are four basic materials in use: Cotton-linen, Dacron, Fiberglass and Aluminum Sheet. (We'll cover the three fabrics in this chapter; see Chapter VI for the aluminum covering.) Each material has certain advantages and disadvantages. All three are applied about the same. We'll call out the differences as we go along.

The most widely used and oldest fabric is either cotton or linen. It gives the smoothest finish for the least amount of dope. Its adhesion is best but its organic nature is subject to more rapid deterioration due to air pollution. There are anti-fungicides which help protect from mildew but not chemical contaminants. Dacron will last twice as long and fiberglass is almost indestructible. Dope adhesion to the latter two is only about one-third as good as with cotton and the weave never seems to be quite filled. The result; a rougher finish, not as shiny. Cotton and linen are water-shrinkable; dacron is heat-shrinkable. Fiberglass must be applied tight since the only shrinkage is what little you can get from the dope.

Another factor with fabric coverings is that little or no experience or tools are needed. Also it's noiseless to work with—which your neighbors will appreciate! All you really need are a few tools which can be purchased in any hardware store or 5&10. A garage or cellar or even your backyard (if it's a calm, warm, dry day) will do for a shop. So make up your mind which you think will be best for your project.

Since this is most likely a spare-time project, you'll need an area big enough to take a wing or fuselage, yet small enough to heat easily for an evening's work during the cold weather. For best results you should be able to maintain a minimum of 60°F with some ventilation.

The covering materials you'll have to get from one of the aviation supply houses, either through your local airport or by mail. *Trade-A-Plane* is the best source, since many companies catering to older aircraft take ads to display their products and wares. If you can't find a copy of *Trade-A-Plane,* send $3.00 to *Trade-A-Plane,* Crossville, Tenn. They'll send you enough paper in a year's time to cover all the walls and ceilings in your house— with enough left over to replace the present tissue you may be using.

Most of the miscellaneous items you will need can be found at the local hardware or five and dime. Make a list: brushes, clamps or clothes pins, a six-inch needle or twelve-inch for wings, masking tape, 'T' pins, tape measure, gallon cans or pails, etc. Then go shopping or have your wife do it (you may wish to get her involved in the beginning, before she demands "equal time"). Don't forget a couple of saw horses and a small stepladder—those dope cans can get mighty unsteady. It will pay you in the long run to get quality brushes. With a little care after each use, they'll outlast cheap brushes and you won't be constantly picking brush hairs off the work.

The most widely used agent to add body and stiffness to fabrics is dope, a cellulose material which is thinned with a highly volatile solvent. After application the solvent evaporates, leaving the cellulose base adhering to the fabric surface. With numerous applications the surface becomes stiff yet flexible. The evaporation of the solvent depends on temperature and, to some extent, on humidity. On a warm, dry day you may find it hard to work fast enough to apply dope before it becomes too difficult to brush on smoothly—it begins to drag and roll up. In this case, more solvent must be added, or even a retarder, to slow the drying or evaporation.

Any form of evaporation requires heat. If the humidity is high you may see a whitish coloration form on the surface. This is known as "blushing." The very rapid evaporation of the solvent causes a large temperature drop on the surface of the dope. It's natural for water vapor to condense on contact with this cool surface, if the surface temperature is at or below the dew point of the surrounding air. The water will evaporate once the surface has warmed but will leave a whitish discoloration and a rough surface. By adding a little dope retarder to slow down the evaporation, the surface temperature doesn't reach the dew point and blushing doesn't occur. In very humid weather you may not be able to stop the blushing. So give up and try another day.

There are two types of dope on the market. Both are used either in combination or indivdually. Nitrate has more adhesion but becomes more brittle with age and is very flammable. Butyrate has slightly less adhesion but remains more flexible with age and is fire-resistant. Current practice is to use nitrate for the initial wrapping and lapping of the primary cover and tapes, plus one or two coats, then butyrate for additional clear, silver and color coats. The number of coats will depend on the finish you want. A high-gloss, hand-rubbed finish may take as many as fifteen or twenty coats.

There are other agents used to add stiffness. Plastic resins have been used with some success. They do add considerable weight but are quite stiff and rigid. Make a survey, yourself, of all the manufacturers' information on various methods. Then find a few ships that have been out in the weather for a few years. You will get some idea of what your ship will look like a couple of years from now.

The covering is the window-dressing and it is worth taking a few extra pains to have the bird do you proud when you land and taxi up to the line.

After you have decided which fabric to use, there are two ways it can be purchased; either by the yard, in various widths up to 90", or as a ready-made envelope, shaped and sewn to fit the various components. The envelopes may cost a bit more but will save time and eliminate the need of sewing seams to FAA specifications (see FAA AC 43.13-1 Chapter 3, Sec. 1 Par. 74). Fabric, being limited in width, will require several seams for large surfaces such as wings and fuselage. The exception is fiberglass. Sewed seams there are impractical because of the loose weave. The material requires a wide overlap, usually around the leading and trailing edges. The material manufacturer will usually have printed instructions explaining the application of, and the FAA requirements for, the use of his material. At any rate check AC 43.13-1 Chapter 3. It will give the details on methods tried and proved over the years as good practice.

There are three or four companies which specialize in envelopes for most of the more popular types (Cessna 120, 140, 170; Ercoupe; Piper, etc.). They list by make, model and year of manufacture. Just order and you'll get the fabric for each component neatly wrapped and ready to slip on.

If it's a home-built, you'll have to buy the yardage you need. Just a thought—you may be able to order a blanket or adapt an envelope that's similar in design and dimension. Send the envelope manufacturer a sketch with dimensions, and he may even make them up for you. At least the seams will be straight, without wrinkles or gathers. It's not easy, believe me, so let a professional do it. If you must sew, make sure it conforms to AC 43.13-1 Chapter 3, Par. 74.

Now you're ready to start! The ship is in the garage . . . the material is ordered . . . all tools you'll need on hand . . . kids in bed . . . wife reading or on the phone. Nobody to disturb you.

As a general rule, all inspection plates, panels, covers, doors, windows, fairings, etc., are removed and labeled (use a piece of masking tape and a marking pencil). All hardware is best replaced where it came from or stored in a marked can. Only remove what might interfere with the recovering. No use doing more than is necessary. Now with knife (razor-type) in hand, cut around the edges of the old envelope, taking care not to scratch or score the metal or wood structure. Keep the old envelope intact as much as possible. You'll need it to show the locations of various inspection holes, screw or stitch patterns, seams, etc.

Now's the time to give the structure, cables, pulleys . . . everything . . . a really thorough inspection. This should be done by a licensed mechanic or FAA inspector, or at least checked by

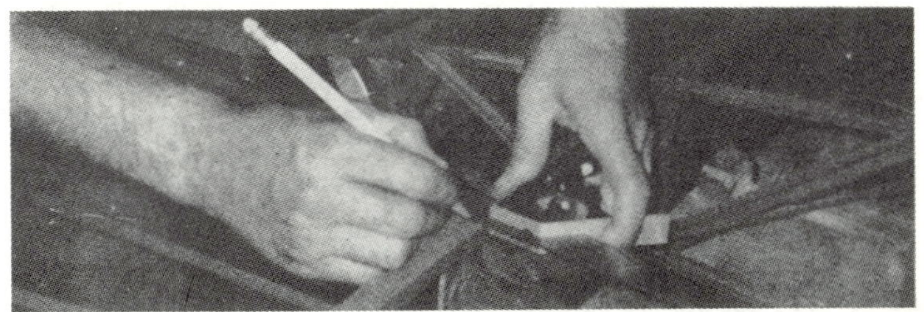

Using a square and pencil to mark off bay for trammeling a wing panel.

one, and a list of non-airworthy items made. Then when these repairs are made either by, or under the supervision of, the mechanic, he'll approve what's been done. You won't find anyone who will sign for work he hasn't seen. Once all the repairs are made and approved, it's a good idea to chromate the structure or varnish the wood. It's the last time for many years that structure can be looked over so well. One additional point: sharp edges should be filed, then covered with masking tape to protect the fabric. Don't forget to dope-proof areas where the fabric will be doped around a member or stringer. Otherwise the dope will remove the chromate at that point and expose it to rapid deterioration. There is a dope-proof paint made just for this purpose.

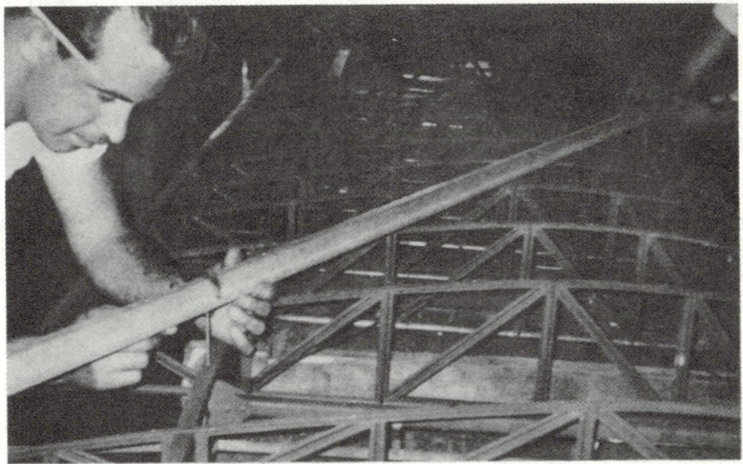

With a long angle, clamps and pointer, this mechanic is checking the rigging on the outboard bay of a Piper Tri-Pacer wing panel.

Most fabric-covered wings are quite flexible to facilitate rigging when installed on the fuselage. But before the covering is installed the internal rigging of the wing panel has to be checked and adjusted. Most wings are square with the fuselage center line (longitudinal axis). Basically, the spars are separated into bays with a compression rib or member forming the structural member between spars. This forms a square or rectangle which, as you know, can collapse easily unless you install a diagonal brace. This brace is most likely a wire. Wires of course work only in tension so you'll have to have two in order to have strength in both directions. Notice also that the heaviest wire is always the one resisting the movement of the wing tip forward.

You may not believe it but a sharp pull-up moves the wing tips forward with far greater force than they'd ever move backward. It's tied in with the center-of-lift moving forward as the angle of attack increases. For a long time no one would believe the old test pilots who survived the loss of wings, that the wings moved forward before they went back and away . . . Let's get back to the rigging.

Sometimes the diagonal is a tube which will take tension and compression. At any rate the wires will have to be adjusted to square up the wing and also the tension of the wires. The illustrations show how this is being done with two pointers clamped to a long rod. By adjusting the wires until the distance is equal for each wire it's got to be square. That is if you've set up equal distances from the center of the fuselage along the spars from one compression member or bay to the other, out to the last one at the tip or near it.

With the trammeling completed and the wires secured, check the control-system cables, pulleys, and fairleads; light wires, pitot and static lines, gas tanks and fuel lines. It would be a shame to have to cut holes in the new fabric just to check or install items which can be done so easily now.

The ship is now ready for the cover. Make a check list of all the materials and necessary tools—then check your list. Now you'll need a friend—your wife, son, or the kid next door—to help slip the cover over the bigger components. Once this is done you will be able to work for the most part by yourself.

Drape the envelope over the structure to get some idea of the fit and where you might have to cut to alter it. Now slip the envelope

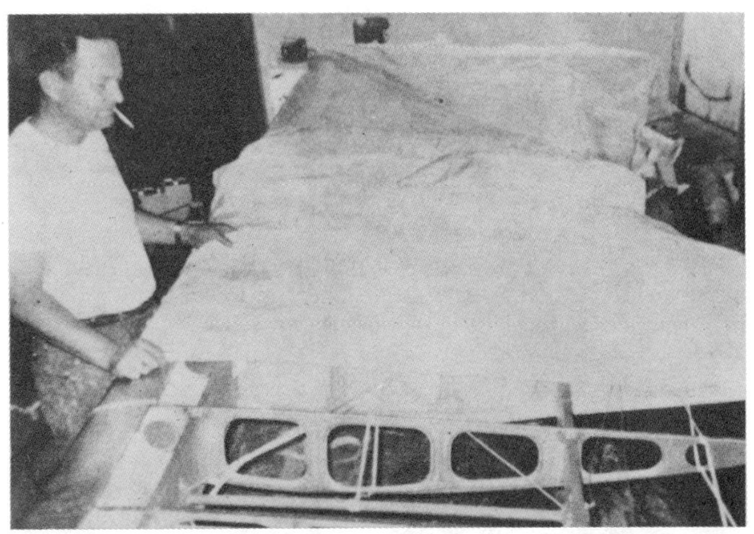

Working envelope of fabric around the panel starting from the tip.

over and around the structure; cut and trim carefully and as little as possible. Note in the illustrations how the envelope didn't fit up the fin. It had to be cut, then slipped over the fin and lapped over the rest of the cover.

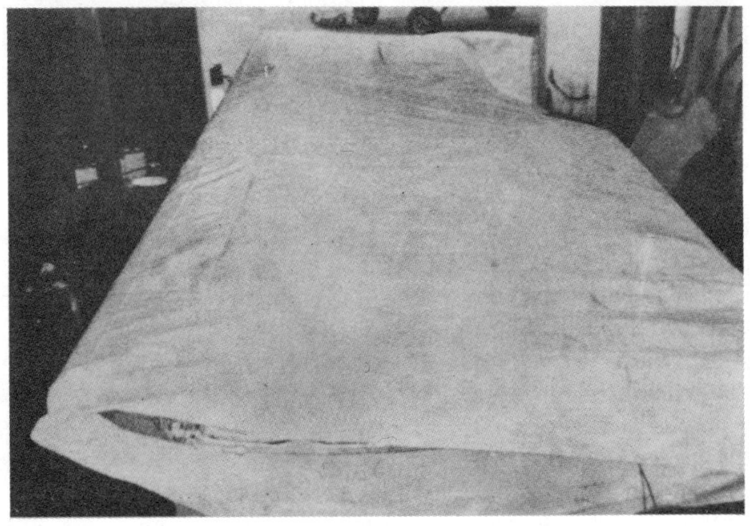

The envelope completely encloses the panel.

The fuselage cover requires a bit of fussing with to get the best fit. Use clamps or clothes pins generously to obtain the best fit. Wings and control surfaces don't have many compound shapes so they are easier to work smooth.

Now cut and glue and trim around windows, gear, tail and door posts (see accompanying illustrations). Use nitrate dope or a fabric cement. This will take time and a few pains but it's where all the good, trim, professional look will come from. Don't be perturbed if you have to pull off the glued area to get a good fit. It happens to the best of us!

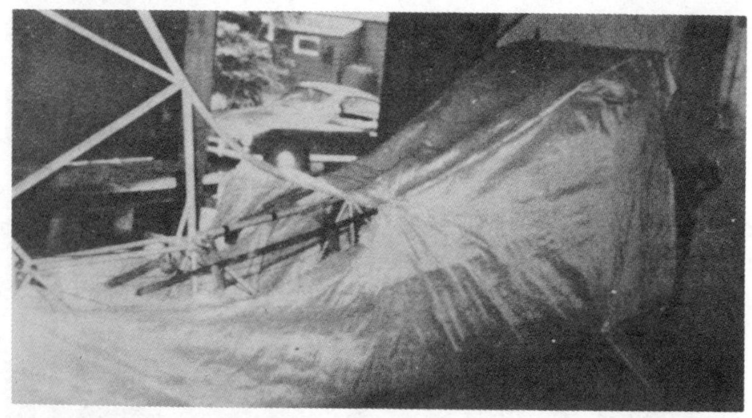

This fuselage envelope had to be cut to slip over the integral fin.

Once you're tied down all around, dampen the cotton-linen to tighten and remove the few wrinkles. Dacron needs heat and your wife's iron has the control to give you the best results. Just keep it moving—use the tip for spots or tight places (see illustration). Fiberglass will stay as you fitted it.

Now mix up a can of half-and-half: one part nitrate dope and one part nitrate thinner. Give the whole component two generous brush-coats. Be careful not to push too much through the weave. In the case of control surfaces, drops may form and drip to the inner surface of the lower side. If allowed to dry, the drip will always show no matter how many coats are applied and sanded.

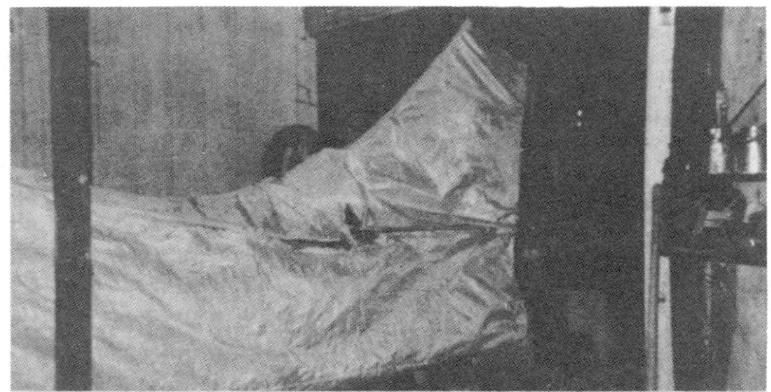

The cutaway fin fabric is rejoined to the fuselage envelope.

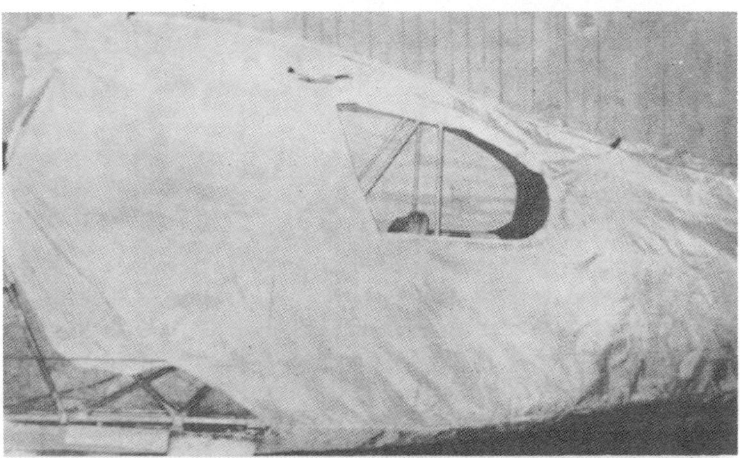

Side view of the fuselage envelope before cutting out forward windows.
Note the rear window has been cut and glued to the frame.

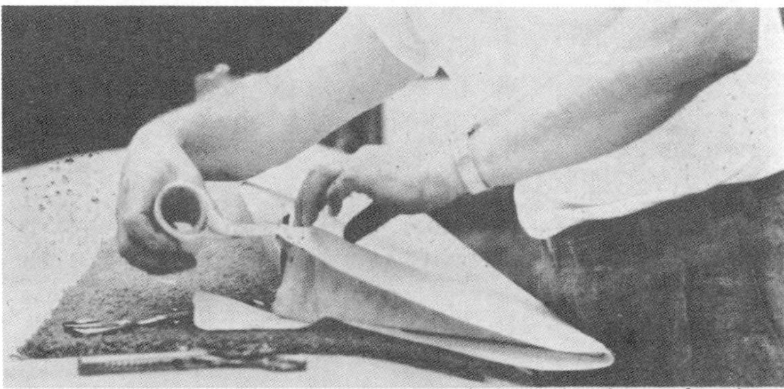

The controls, such as this aileron, require fitting, trimming and patience
around the edges.

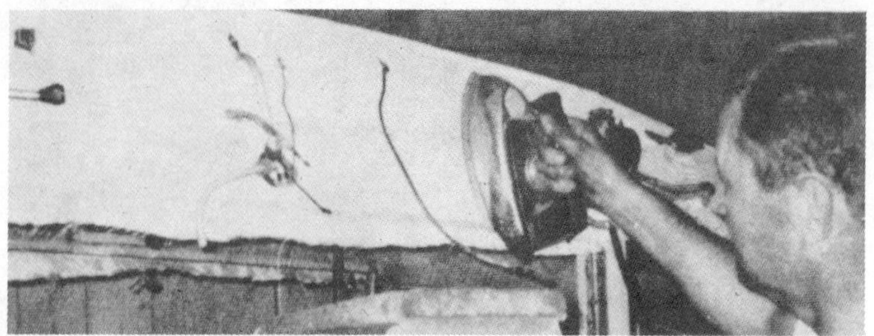

Using our wife's favorite iron, we work this dacron fabric to a tight fit
around the wing fittings.

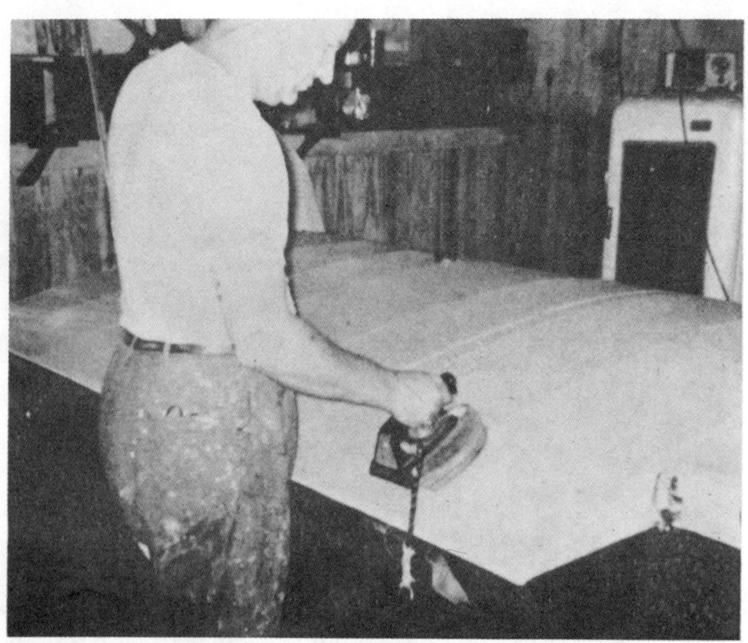

Here again the iron is used on the wing surface to smooth out the
wrinkles and tighten up the envelope of dacron.

Now you're ready for the reinforcement tapes. Wings and control surfaces and usually the fin will require some form of attachment to the ribs or structure. Here's where the old covering is used for reference. Either position the old fabric as it was originally and mark each point, or use a ruler to lay out the pattern. Use a soft lead pencil, *never* an ink-type marking pencil (it will bleed through any dope or paint). The type of attachment varies—screws, cord, clips, rivets. Use the original method selected by the manufacturer.

Before the attachments are made, reinforcement tape is doped in place. Use a short piece ½" long as on tail surface or the length of each rib for a wing. Where rib stitch cord is used through the wing and around the rib, remember the reinforcement tape must be applied to both top and bottom surfaces.

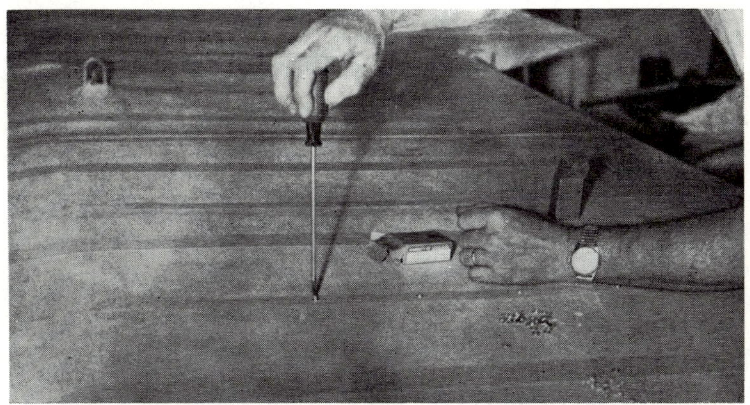

Use of washers and screws to attach fabric to ribs of the wing.

With the rib stitching completed, you are ready to install pinked tapes. A general rule is to apply tapes over all rib stitching along all ribs; around leading and trailing edges, longerons and stringers first; then along trailing edge, tip and butt ribs for wings; completely around the ends of tail surfaces from aft forward so all laps are downwind; same for fin and fuselage, then around doors, windows, windshield, gear, etc.

Lay out and cut as many tapes as would be convenient to handle. One at a time would take too long; too many would make storing and finding a problem—plus the fact that they'd get dirty and wrinkled which would show when finished.

Each tape is started by laying three or four inches of dope the width of the tape at the point you wish to start each tape. Then position tape, rubbing with the fingertips until the dope soaks through. Then brush more dope over this same area. Allow this to set so that slight tension can be applied to the tape. It may take a few minutes or so—depending on drying conditions. You might start a couple at a time or go from one end of a wing to the other. Once tacked, apply a tape-width of dope along the area to be taped. Stretch the tape slightly, rub down with fingers or brush, making sure tape is thoroughly wet, then brush a coat of dope over the tape. After a few tries you'll find out how much, and how far you can go. One point: near the end of the tape, use the pinking shears to finish the edge. In fact all edges of exposed tape should be pinked.

Fabric tapes are applied to the back side of this wing and wrap around the leading edge.

With the taping finished you've only got to dope on the inspection rings, drain grommets, etc. Again check the old fabric or check another ship of the same make and model. As a last resort, call your mechanic and ask his advice. At this point the surface will require a once-over-lightly with 320 (grit) wet-or-dry, dry preferred. Stay off the rib stitching, screws, any high points—or you'll be using more tape.

The hard job's done now. Just work in three or four more clear coats. Use about 25% thinner to get a faster build-up, but, again, this will depend on conditions. Straight dope may be used when it

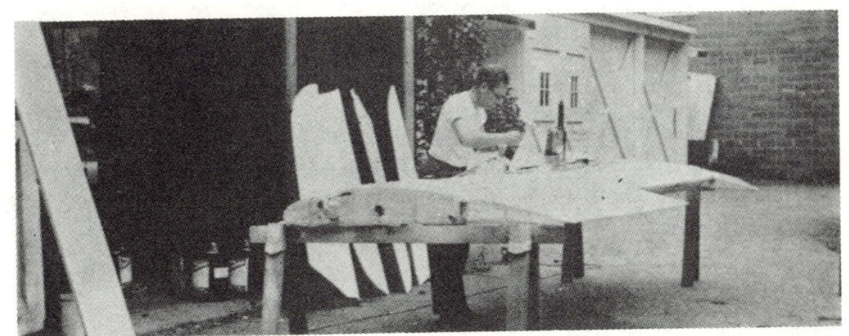

A calm Saturday and an ideal day to get a lot of work done on the surfaces.

doesn't drag and you'll get a shiny surface with fewer coats. Usually the surface is smooth but if it happens to be rough, light dry sanding is in order.

Now you're ready to apply silver dope. Mix your own or buy ready-mixed. (It's only aluminum powder mixed with clear dope.) Mix powder with a little thinner to make a thin paste, then add to uncut dope. Mix thoroughly. This method will eliminate your sediment problems.

Generally you'll get better results with spraying than with brushing. It will save you all kinds of sanding time. Spray gun, hose and a small portable compressor can be borrowed, rented or even bought quite reasonably. Professional equipment isn't needed to do a good job. Just get some advice and guidance from your mechanic friend and play around with the equipment a bit. You'll be surprised how quickly it will come to you. I suggest that you stop in at your local auto parts store. They not only sell paint, but can also give or sell you a booklet on how to paint. Since some parts of the ship will require lacquer or enamel, you'll find the store will be glad to help.

Dope for spraying will have to be thinned anywhere from 1-to-1 or 2-to-1 with thinner. You should get quite a fog. Shoot at a piece of paper or metal. Adjust the fan to the width of four fingers outstretched. The fluid flow should be enough to be wet, yet break up to look like very fine sand grains, the finer the better. Once this pattern is obtained, you can control the quantity of material you put on the surface by the speed of movement (assuming a 50% overlap of the fan width). Too slow and you'll get runs—too fast and it'll be dry. Ideally, move just fast enough to avoid runs. This

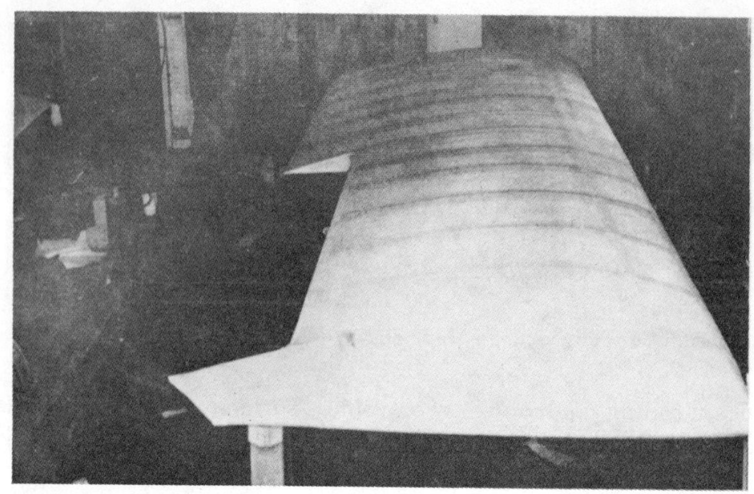

Heres a panel ready to be painted with silver and then the final color.

With a tight envelope taped, all we need is a few more brush coats and the fuselage will be ready for the silver.

You can see how the tapes are placed over the longerons and stringers, also extra tape where piecing had to be done to join the fin to the main envelope.

way you'll get a maximum wet coat with constant color.

Generally, you apply clear coats until you've just about got the finish you want. Then wet sand the entire surface before spraying silver. Make sure the surface is dry and wipe off dust before spraying. About two cross-coats (a cross-coat is once-over from left to right and then fore and aft or up and down) is sufficient, but you may wish to wet sand again then spray on a couple more cross-coats for a better, glossier finish.

Finally the color—two wet cross-coats will give you a full color. Usually the light colors are sprayed first but this order is important only if the first color may bleed through the second. Blushing must be avoided with the color. Either use retarder or wait for less humid conditions.

A little planning of the colors used in the design may save you many hours of needless masking. If a simple striping and the registration numbers are to be one color, paint this color first. Then you'll have only this to mask off, instead of the whole ship.

Masking of a design is an art in itself but you can do quite well if you take the time with basic details. Use paper patterns to lay out and duplicate a design from one side to the other. "Eyeball" your straight lines. See that all curved lines "fair" well. Rough out the design with tape on one side. Don't rub the tape down, so it will come off easily.

This young man is helping out by sanding the fin carefully at the rib stitch points. Correct sanding will give a shinier finish.

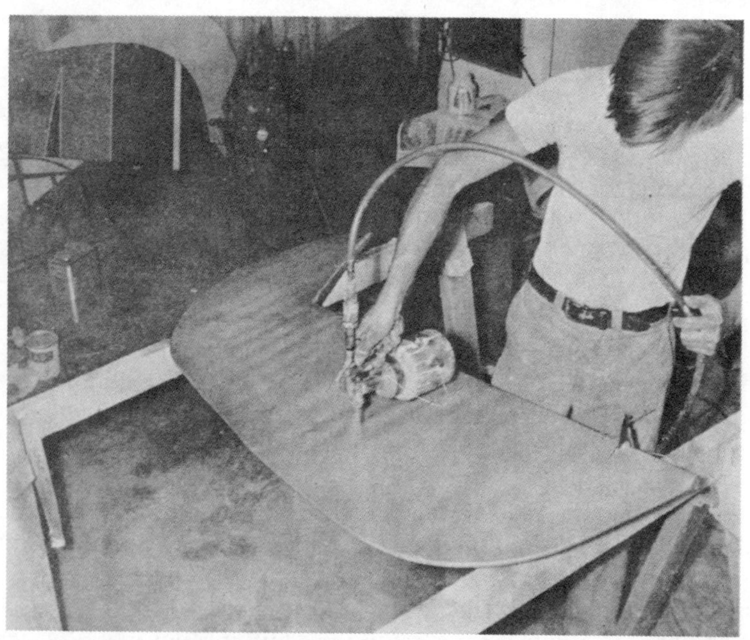

Young helper gets in the act with a couple of cross-coats of silver on this nearly completed rudder.

When you get it the way you'd like, then take pains with the "faired" curves and straight lines. Rub the tape down and use a fingernail to lay down tape over rivet heads, seams, plates, etc.

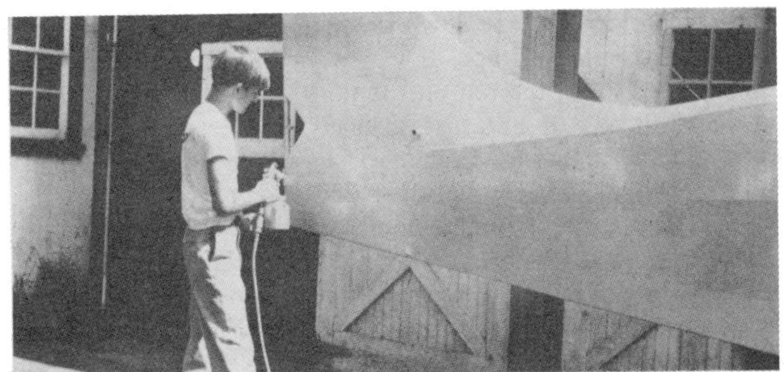

Out in the sun, helper Pete Lloyd has to work fast while spraying the first coat of color on the fuselage.

Registration numbers can be laid out with this tape but a better deal is die-cut masks. They are cheap and right to regulations. Also you can place the whole set of numbers in position before removing the protective backing. If they are not in position, you can move them around until they are.

Once you have everything laid out, mask off all but what is to be painted with old newspaper or buy a roll of wrapping paper. The answer to a good masking job is the complete sealing of all areas and checking to see that you haven't missed any areas. A small tear or missed spot can mess up an otherwise perfect job.

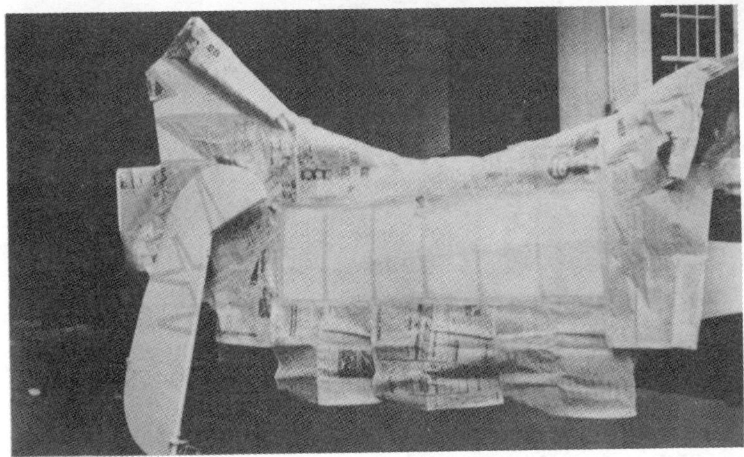

Newspaper is ideal for masking off the numbers and design for the second color.

It's a good idea to wipe down the area to be masked. Dust will inhibit the adhesion of tape. If you want sharp edges, keep your tape clean—putting the roll on the floor or a dusty bench means the edges will pick up lint, dirt, hair, etc. It's best to paint as soon as possible after masking. As the tape ages, it grows on the surface resulting in possible peeling of the paint. A day or two is okay but a week or more can give you trouble. And don't ever leave the tape on out in the rain or sun—you'll have to scrape it off.

After you've painted the second or more colors, remove the tape around the painted area at least, just as soon as it sets up a bit. When pulling off tape it's best to pull back along the tape and toward the new paint. This will avoid most lifting of underpaint and cobwebbing along the edges. You'll most likely have to use enamel on metal and dope on fabric or you can use lacquer on both.

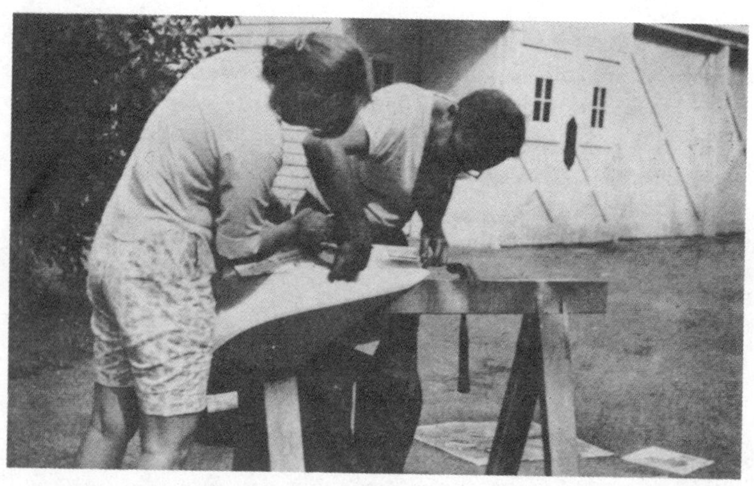

Mom helped when it came to masking off the wheel fairings.

Once the paint job is finished you usually feel a real sense of accomplishment and rightly so—it took many painstaking hours getting to this point; but it's worth it.

Windows

The only glazing materials in general use for small aircraft today are the acrylic plastics, and, rarely, glass or safety glass. The acrylics offer such all-round satisfactory properties that they have almost entirely displaced other materials.

Available under several trade names, these plastics can be cut by sawing and sanding, and they are formed to complex shapes when heated. As a result, they can be successfully used by the amateur in original construction or in repairs to existing aircraft. The materials are cast to size in sheets of standard thicknesses. Most commonly used are the .090, .120, .187, and .250 sizes.

Usually the sheets are furnished with protective, self-adhesive paper covering on both sides. Because the materials are soft, the covering should be left in place until the last possible moment before installation. Patterns for cutting or trim can be drawn right on the covering, and the parts can be cut out before the paper is removed, provided the parts are not to be formed.

All flat and single-curvature panels can be made without heating, unless a flange requires a sharp bend, or the contour is extremely sharp—as it might be for a leading edge, landing-light cover, for example. If heat is required for a bend, the protective covering must be removed before the part is heated since the adhesive can damage the surface at high temperatures.

Plastic panels expand as the temperature increases, much more than metals do, so it is necessary to allow room for this expansion. If the panel is mounted in a snap-in rubber bead, no other precaution is required. However, if the piece is supported in a metal frame, the plastic must be cut undersize. About .10 inches all around is right for a side window of average size, more for larger panels. Any holes through the plastic for screws or bolts should be oversize to allow the same amount for expansion as the clearance around the edges. Where a metal frame is used, the plastic should be cushioned by a soft gasket on both sides.

Parts that are bent too sharply for cold flexing, or that have compound curvature may be formed at a temperature of 275°F. This can be obtained in a cooking oven, or in mineral oil near its boiling temperature. If an oven is used, the thermostat should be checked first against a good thermometer, and the part should be heated with the door tightly closed to insure uniform heating. Temperature must be held at the desired level about five minutes for each 1/16 inch thickness of the plastic, to be sure it is up to forming temperature all the way through.

The plastic should be supported on a sheet of metal or hard-board if it is more than six inches or so wide, so as to avoid sagging that might affect the final contours. It must be handled carefully in the soft condition, as the lightest touch can mar the surface or induce strains which impair the optical quality. Plenty of material should be left around the edges for holding and clamping over the form. Clean cotton work gloves usually give adequate protection for the hands, and minimize surface marking.

While the acrylics can be readily formed with air pressure, the better method for non-professional use is the solid form. The form can be any convenient material such as wood or plaster, and should be covered with a very soft felt about 1/16 inch thick. As soon as the plastic sheet comes from the oven or heating bath, it is quickly drawn over the form by hand, stretching into the shape of the tool. If the material stiffens before it is completely formed, it can be reheated, and should be supported so that it tends to sag in the direction of forming. The part should be allowed to cool to room temperature on the form.

It is important that only gentle pressure be applied when form-ing the acrylics. Too much will cause the soft surface to pick up the texture of the tool. Enough help should be on hand to have a grip on the edge of the sheet about every 18 inches. There are tricks and "feel" to this, as there are to any complicated operation. Con-sequently, it pays to use a little scrap material for practice. Even a few corner pieces trimmed off the workpiece will serve the pur-pose, and may save a good deal of expense.

Acrylics can be joined by cementing where it is necessary to reinforce or repair. The cement can be obtained from the manu-facturer, or from most aircraft supply houses. The cement is a solvent, and the joint is made by softening the plastic and pressing the surfaces together, holding them under pressure until the solvent has evaporated.

Cutting or drilling plastics can be done with typical woodwork-ing tools, except that finer-tooth saw blades are used. The plastic is brittle, and needs more support than wood. A piece of plywood or hardboard on each side is best. Because friction softens the plastic, it is advisable to withdraw the drill frequently for cooling, and to interrupt saw cuts or use a faster feed than in cutting wood.

Cracks may be repaired in acrylics much the same as in wood. First, they are stop-drilled, then a patch is cemented over the crack area, using a bevelled edge all around. A patch can be inserted and cemented in place of a damaged area, also. However, only a relatively small area should be patched, and no repairs should be made in the parts of windshield or windows in the pilot's direct line of sight for normal operations.

Minor surface scratches may be polished out with a very fine abrasive such as jeweler's rouge or an automotive rubbing compound. The surface should be cleaned with a mild soap and water, or with one of the proprietary cleaners, but never with any other solvents. A protective coat of clear wax is recommended to reduce surface wear and tear.

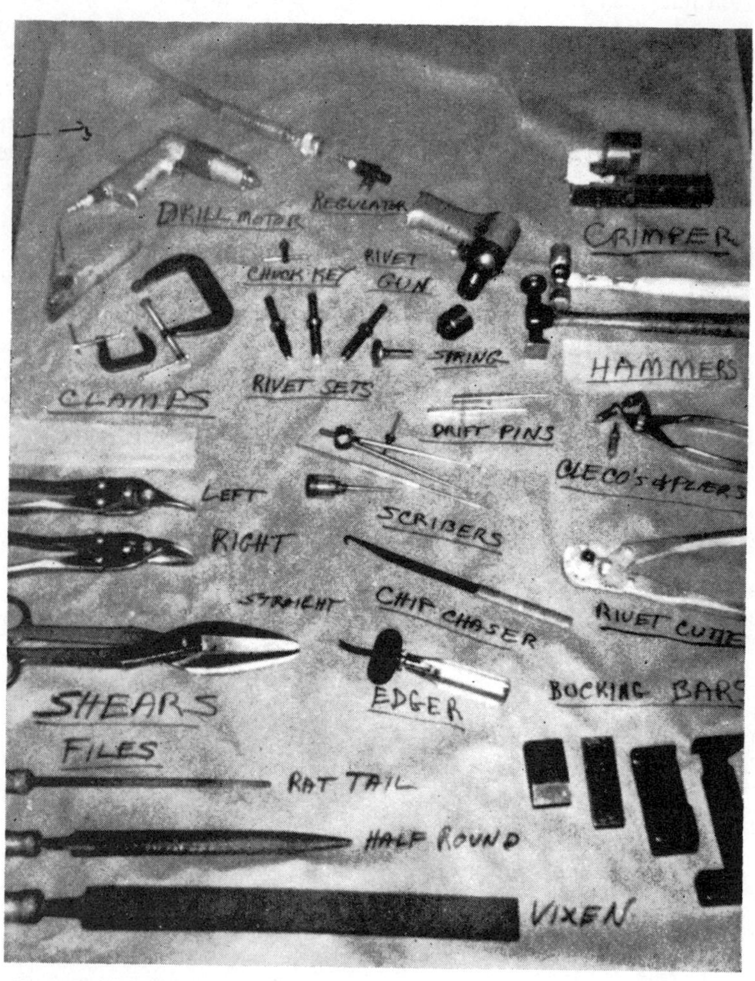

A composite view of most of the tools (hand) used in sheet-metal work.

5. What's the Mystery in Working Sheet Metal?

Why is it that sheet metal construction and repair is held in such awe by those who have not tried it? It need not be so. Granted, it does take a few tools that you won't find around the house—but those that you do need are easy to come by. Of course, you also need some mechanical skill and an awareness of quality. But with a little practice and patience, you will find that you can acquire a degree of skill which will be acceptable and which will give you a great deal of personal satisfaction.

Your friend, the A&P mechanic, should be consulted. In fact, he's the one who will judge your skill. First, though, let's give you a little background so you can talk to him about your metal work and be on his wave length.

In an accompanying illustration are all the hand tools needed to do the job. You can buy all of these tools, which can run into mucho bucks, or you can borrow some of the more expensive ones, such as the rivet gun and drill motor. Your A&P friend can help you here—ask him!

The *drill* is usually electric, unless you have a good supply of compressed air. A 1/4" chuck is good enough. Anything larger would be unwieldy and too tiring to work with.

Make sure the cord is in good condition to avoid a shocking experience. The use of a grounding plug will help. It is desirable, but not essential, to be able to control the speed of the drill. Air drills have always had this control but only recently has this been available for the electric drill.

The *rivet gun* is air-operated. You'll need about 80 lbs. A small two-stage compressor will do because you won't need a large volume of air, but the pressure is important. Most of the repairs on light

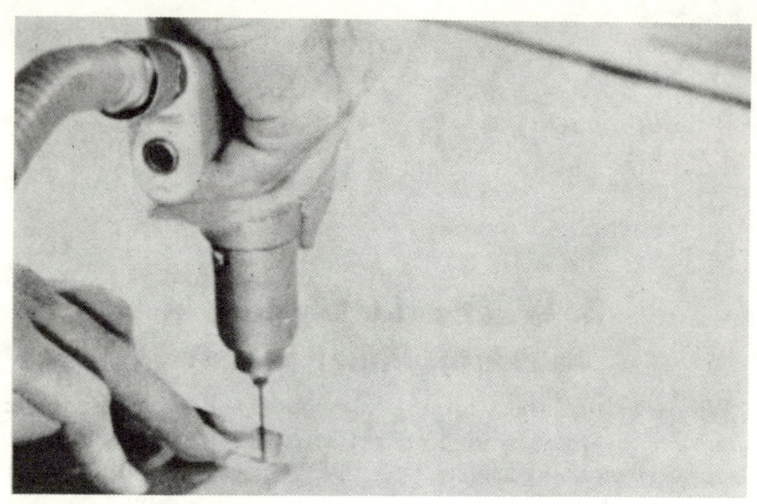

Holding the drill properly is all-important.

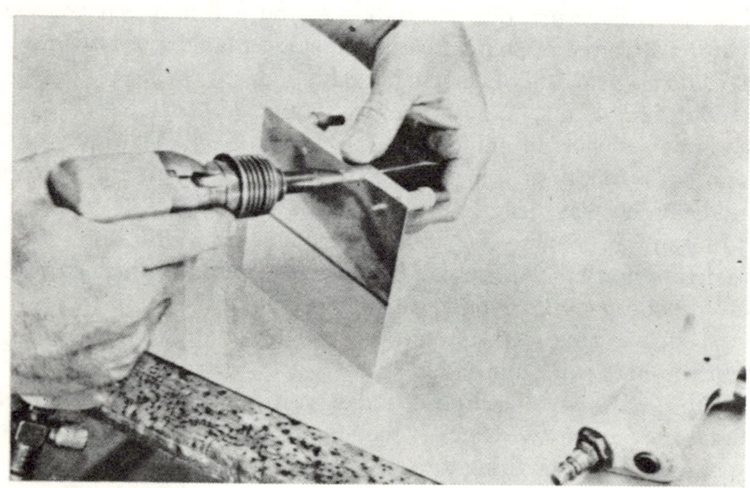

Riveting requires the co-ordination of fingers as well as hands.

planes require a gun which will take from 3/32″ to 5/32″ rivets. It is the short-barrelled type usually designated as an OY. It hits with a short rapid stroke which doesn't require a heavy bucking bar and doesn't dent the area around the rivet in thin skins. When ⅜″ rivets are to be used you'll have to get a longer stroke gun which hits slower but harder. Usually you have an air regulator in between the air supply and the gun. This allows you to set the pressure at full trigger for the size and length rivet you may be shooting in a series. This means you'll get a consistent bucked head by holding full trigger for a given length of time. You'll find a

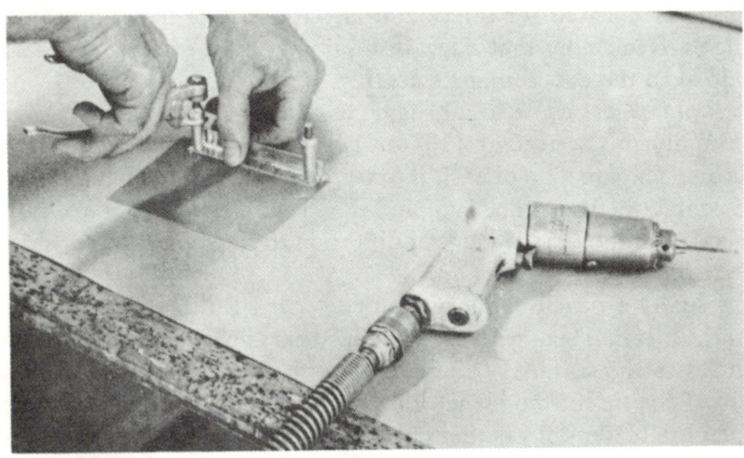

Cleco-type sheet holders are indispensable for sheet-metal work.

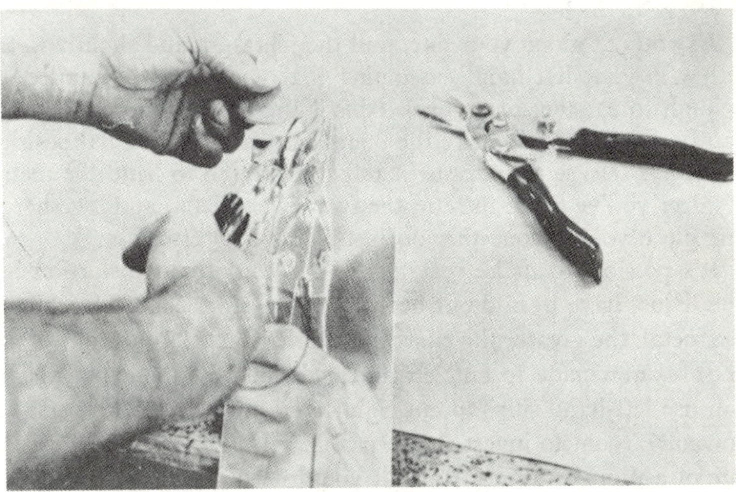

Using left-hand snips, this worker is cutting a hole in a piece of skin prior to locating it on the structure.

rhythm will develop and you'll sense just how long to squeeze the trigger. You will also learn to finger the trigger to control the operation of the gun. Here you may be pushing the rivet to get the head down, or indicating to the bar man which rivet you're on, or giving a light tap to draw the skins tight before final setting. With the gun are appropriate rivet sets and a retaining spring. This spring is essential for safety and also for ease of handling at odd angles. Remember that a few drops of oil added every so often will help keep the gun running smoothly.

Hand shears come in all shapes and sizes. Three basic types are normally used: straight (10" or 12"), and left and right curved shears. The function of each is to cut or shear the metal at the point of contact between the metal and the shear. The object is to cut the metal with the least amount of distortion to the dimensions or shape desired.

Usually a pencil or sharp-pointed scriber is used to mark a line on the metal. Then, with the straight shears held vertical or at right angles to the surface of the cut, start the cut. Cut only to within ¼" of the tips of the blades, then slide the shear up the cut as you open the blades for another cut. Watch the scribe line as you close the blades. You can guide the cut along the line by tilting the shear slightly to the left, if you're on the right of the line, or to the right, if you're to the left.

As you cut along your line, pull the metal up and slightly to the left with your left hand (assuming that you are right-handed)— enough to use the spring-back (this is the amount of bending that can be done and still have the metal return to its original position after you release the pressure) but not enough to bend the metal. If, after you've made the cut, the two pieces lie flat and together as one piece you've done the job just right—no distortion.

It's possible to make very gentle curves without distortion but you'll just have to find out how much by experience. The thinner the metal, the greater the curve allowable. The left and right shears or snips are made to cut left and right curves. Incidentally, you can use left-hand snips to cut right-hand curves (or vice versa) if you have room to invert the snips. These snips can cut a hole the size of a dime on thin metal but you'll need a starting hole about ¼" in diameter. Insert the ends or nose of the blade in the hole just enough to work the blades. Cut only a small bit at a time;

never close the blades so far they meet. As you work the blades, turn the snips as you cut. Cut inside your scribe line and slowly work toward it in ever widening circles, pulling the scrap metal out of the way as you cut. This will reduce the distortion to a minimum.

If you are cutting out a larger hole, a larger center piece may be cut out of the center, but always work to within a 1/4" or less before the final cut. Generally, then, the smaller the radius you're cutting to, the closer you'll have to work to the nose of the snips. Cutting to the outside of a line such as an inspection cover you would use the same procedure but it's not necessary to work so close to the nose of the snips.

The same general procedure would be used when cutting or trimming a curved part such as a cowling or formed wing tip. Work the snips or shears toward the scrap and away from the part. Take smaller and smaller cuts as you near your scribe line. This will give you the least amount of distortion.

Cutting, especially in soft annealed metal, may leave an edge. This can be filed or, to make it easier, use an edger designed for the purpose. And to give a more professional look, crimp the edges with a hand crimper.

Drill bits come in all sizes and shapes, too. But you'll need only a few for most repairs and metal construction. The home craftsman is familiar with fractional drill sizes, but aircraft uses require a closer tolerance so we turn to number drills. These give you a step of a few thousandths of an inch between each number. You can then select a number drill to fit the close tolerance required on bolts and rivets. Each rivet has an optimum or nominal drill size. You'll need only five or six sizes for the rivets you'll use: 3/32"—#40, .098; 1/8"—#30, .128; 5/32"—#21, .159; 3/16"—#12, .189. Note that the number is high for the small diameter. You'll generally use these sizes for removing or drilling out rivets during a repair.

Number drills can be purchased from hardware stores, auto supply or industrial supply houses in most cities. Just ask for high-speed, jobbers'-length drills by the numbers.

Two additional drill forms which are useful in aircraft repair or construction are the router bit and counter sink. These may have to be ordered for you by the local supplier. The router bit

Shown here are hand-operated shrinker and stretcher which forms small angles into complicated shapes.

has a drill point to start a hole but its primary use is to cut or rout irregular shapes down to its own diameter—easily, quickly, and with no distortion of the surrounding metal. It works best at higher rpm's but a regular drill will do fine. Caution should be taken to reduce injury. Always position the work so that you are working away from yourself and your fingers. The countersink is a short, wide drill bit usually with a 1/4″ shank to fit the average drill motor. Its use is special: to cut a tapered hole to fit the head of a flush rivet (AN426) or flush screw head. Its rake or taper is usually 100° —the same as the flush rivet. A stop countersink is a refinement which allows you to pre-set the depth of the taper where you're going to set a number of flush rivets all the same size.

The *sheet edger* is a hardened rod set in a handle at one end with a sharp V cut in the other end. The V is drawn with moderate pressure along the edge of the sheet. It cuts and thus tapers the edge, much like the old-type knife sharpener works. Once or twice along the edge is enough.

58

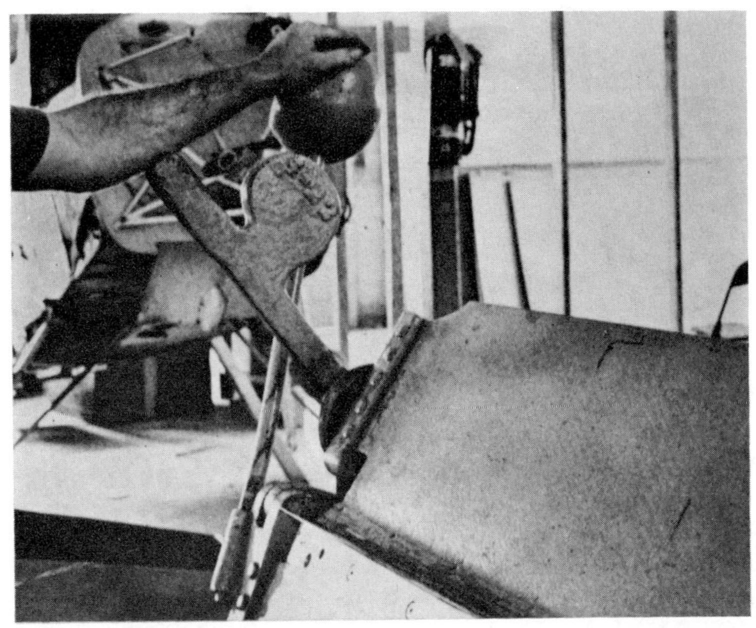

This is a large 8′ leaf brake used to form long bends in thin sheets of metal.

Files are familiar to almost everyone, so just remember to use a semi-fine half-round and/or a rat tail. A flat, long (12″ to 15″) vixen also comes in handy at times.

The *chip chaser* is useful but hard to find. However, you can make one from an old feeler gauge or similar thin (.005 to .010) strip of spring steel. File a small hook in the end and fashion a handle. It's a mighty handy little gadget for getting drilled chips out from between two skins when it's difficult to get them apart before riveting.

Clecos, and the *pliers* to handle them, are indispensable tools to hold skins, angles, frames, ribs, etc. in position while locating and riveting structures large and small. They're made to fit the size of the rivet you're using, or going to use, and can be inserted and removed as many times as needed almost instantaneously. A whole wing or fuselage can be assembled with Clecos before you ever shoot a rivet.

A small foot shear will do a fine job for straight cuts or trimming light gauges of metal.

Rivet sets come in all shapes and sizes. Generally you will need the universal (AN470) and flat head (AN426). The universals would be 3/32″, ⅛″, 5/32″, etc., so about four sets will cover what you'll need for most repairs on light planes.

Clamps, drift pins, and *scribers,* of course need no discussion.

The *rivet cutter* is a handle tool. Its use is to cut most common size rivets to the desired length.

Hammers—without 'em, everything would stop or never be built! Have one smaller than a claw hammer but larger than a tack hammer. The metal finishing hammer is most used with metal as is the plastic-rubber-topped mallet. Of course the ball peen has its place also, for tapping out small dents or stretching a flange.

Bucking bars are the other end of the riveting twosome. The shape and size are limited only by the needs of the job. A block of tool steel or a leaf from an old spring can be fashioned to the shape or angle you need to get on the rivet squarely and solidly.

The *crimper* is a gadget used to bend the edge of the metal to a degree so as to reduce the gaps between rivets at a seam. The one shown here is adjustable in depth and width. It consists of two rollers shaped so as to put a small bend at the very edge of the metal. Because of these rollers, you can pull the crimper along the edge of the metal and very quickly get the edge crimp to close the gaps. It's used before the skins are assembled.

That just about covers most of the hand tools you will need for routine metal work.

The use of the drill may seem simple at first—just push until you're through—BUT, like many seemingly simple operations, it's simple only to the experienced. Even with the best of tooling and support of the parts and pieces in a metal structure, the drilling becomes the most important operation.

Crooked, elongated, misaligned, oversize holes will result in poor fitting, uneven, buckled joints, and seams which will show as ripples and oil cans in skins and gaps between rivets. Swelling of rivets between parts will affect the strength of a joint. Poor holes will also make it difficult to shoot rivets properly.

Here a bar folder is used to set up bends not requiring more than 1″ flanges. It lends itself to accurate repeat operations where uniformity is necessary.

In using the drill, there are several important points to keep in mind. First, the drill motor and drill bit must run true. Make sure the bit is tight in the chuck and that the bit you use is sharp.

Second, hold the drill firmly with one hand and guide it with the other. The guide hand isn't always needed but should be used where control of hole depth is necessary.

How to drill a hole: First, start the point by hand, spinning the chuck or fingering the trigger. A bit turning at low speed is less likely to walk out of position and score the skin. Once the hole is started the drill will hold position. Parts must be held in close contact at the point of drilling from the start of the operation, during the run of the drill until breakthrough and, also important, the withdrawing of the drill. It is in this last movement that most elongation will take place. Since there is no pressure at the drill point once the drill is through the material, the parts will tend to separate. Of course, the better the initial fit the less this will occur but you will always have this condition to some extent. Second, the drill must be held at right angles to the surface. It sounds easy, sure, but . . . it's the nature of aircraft that very little is straight up and down or horizontal. As you're drilling a series of holes around the frame of the fuselage or rib of a wing, you're constantly changing the position of the drill in your hand. The only position that doesn't or shouldn't change is the angle of the drill to the surface of the structure at the point of drilling.

How does one tell the right position or angle? It's quite obvious that you can't check the drill with a protractor before you drill each hole. The eye, though, is an excellent judge of comparison at close range. So by comparing the surface around the drill you can judge the equi-distance required for squareness. If the metal surface is shiny, it's easy. Check the reflection of the drill from two different positions and move the drill parallel to the reflections. After a bit of experience and constant checking, you will find that proper positioning of the drill becomes automatic.

Riveting is somewhat like drilling; only the tool and the purpose are different. You must be at right angles to the surface no matter how odd it may seem. The rivet gun is a hammer—a fast-hitting one. The head is in the gun being pushed against the rivet set many times a second by air pressure. This force is transmitted through the set to the rivet head.

When a bar of hard metal, such as steel, is positioned squarely at the other end of the rivet, this force meets an immovable object. The rivet, being of softer material, starts to spread as it is squeezed between the rivet set and the bucking bar. The whole shank of the rivet spreads. That part passing through the metal swells to fill the drilled hole in the metal. That part beyond the hole is unrestricted and spreads out between the bucking bar and the inner surface of the metal. This becomes the bucked head.

The flowing rivet material fills the hole so completely that the metal pieces cannot move. The two heads hold the metal pieces together like a nut and bolt—only better. It can't come loose by vibration until either its fatigue life or sheer strength have been exceeded.

Long ago it was determined that the rivet shank should extend through the hole to at least $1\frac{1}{2}$ times its diameter in order to have enough material to form a bucked head at least $\frac{1}{2}$-a-diameter thick and $1\frac{1}{2}$-a-diameter wide, in order to give the optimum strength in service. Experience with repairs has shown, however, that the rivet should extend through the hole of a *removed* rivet at least 2 diameters instead of $1\frac{1}{2}$. The reason is that the first driven rivet and the removal of that rivet caused the hole to expand to some degree, thus requiring a bit more material for the second rivet to fill the hole and still get the required $\frac{1}{2}$-by-$1\frac{1}{2}$ bucked head.

Now that we know what the tools are and what their basic functions are, let's use them! Take a few pieces of metal, bend an angle (say $\frac{1}{2}$ x $\frac{1}{2}$ x $90°$) on one, put the two edge-to-edge and drill a No. 40 hole at one end. Make sure you position the hole so as to give at least a 2D (diameter) edge distance from all edges. Secure with a Cleco. Do the same at the other end. Then space holes about 2″ apart from one end to the other. Now clamp the pieces in a vise vertically so that you can insert rivets and can see both sides while you're shooting the rivets. Now practice bucking rivets until you get the feel of the tools. It will take time, of course, but you'll get a great deal of satisfaction when they all look like factory jobs.

Try making a box or two, bending up the metal so that the corners meet, the edges are straight, the bend radius is 3 or 4 times the metal thickness, the rivets are all shot even and to the right degree. You can always use the boxes for rivets or other hardware, so don't throw them away—unless you'd rather not show

Here's an example of the sheet metal covering application for a fabric aircraft. Note the large hole designed for easy access to the tail.

Shown here is a close-up of some of the most frequently used sheet-metal tools.

your handiwork until you're proud of it.

Finally you'll be ready to make those repairs on the wing tip that somehow got too close to the ground (guess the wind was a bit gusty that day?). First look over the job and figure what needs to be done and the easiest way to do it. Remember, somebody put it together, so all you have to do is to figure out how he did it, and then back-track! You'll be surprised at the time you can save and the unnecessary work you can avoid, with a little forethought and a few notes or sketches.

Once you've decided how the job is to be done—order all the parts. When you've got them all, then gather your tools within working distance. Now you're ready to start!

Most repairs involve the replacement of parts (skins, frames, ribs, spars, stringers, etc.) where they're bent and distorted but still roughly intact. If care is taken in removing these parts they can be used as templates, either to fabricate new parts such as flat skins (which do not have compound curves but, rather, simple, large radius bends) or to locate pilot holes in new parts from the factory. Many, or at least most, factory parts have some pilot holes. Of course you may wish to make new parts for various reasons, but you must be able to prove that they are equal to, or better than, the old original parts.

Flat skins are no problem—just use the correct thickness and specs as called for in the manufacturer's repair manual or by inspection of the old parts. Frames, ribs, etc., are much more difficult to fabricate and are cheaper to buy than to make.

Take time to remove damaged parts, or good parts which must be removed, carefully. Drill off the rivet heads, then tap out the shanks with a drift pin. Sometimes this isn't practical due to the thin skins or ribs. Sometimes having a third hand to back up alongside the shank with a bucking bar will help. If this isn't practical, then drill out the whole rivet. If you are working at the edge, a pair of pliers next to the rivet will make the removal go much easier.

With all the parts removed, some can be straightened or reinforced—if the book says so. Make it a rule to save all parts (damaged or otherwise) until the job is completed; you may need them for reference. What if your inspector wants to see if you have the right parts or if he wants to check dimensions?

A typical repair might be the replacement of a tip spar or ribs. Alignment is a problem but by transferring the attachment holes from the old to the new, you will be able to maintain the same alignment as the original spar. If you are very careful you'll find you can Cleco the part in place and the rivets will fit with a minimum of reaming.

With flat skins, first pound out most of the dents. The more severe wrinkles or tears can be cut out entirely but not so much as to lose the original position of the rivet holes. Integral edge stiffening can be tapped out slightly so that they fit or lie over the new part. You'll have to allow for a radius or other curves.

Flatten both the new and the old skins together by using weights such as boards or bricks or anything heavy which will hold the two in position. Never try to bend the skins beyond their spring-back point. This will distort them so that they'll be out of contour unless you bend them back to the original position— which isn't a good idea. It will reduce the fatigue life of the metal and on skin-stressed wings, it may affect the structural strength dangerously.

Once you've lined up the pilot holes, and checked the distance all around, then transfer the holes you feel are needed— first to line up the structure and secondly to give you the rivet pattern. The latter can be done with a marking pencil rather than with a drill. One point here—no matter how carefully the rivets are removed, the holes are always a bit oversize. Usually you can judge the center of the original rivet by the mark it leaves on the old skin. Using this as a guide, drill most of the holes with an undersize drill. The holes you'll use for alignment should be the original size. Naturally, if a hole is oversize you will have to drill out to the next size rivet later. You'll be surprised at how well this method works.

Time is a factor to keep in mind when making a repair. If you take only a day or two to complete a repair, then your memory will serve you well enough, but if the days run into weeks or even months you'd do well to take some notes and pictures, or make a few sketches. Taping parts together and storing everything in one place will save many, many hours of hunting for pieces and parts later.

To *jig* sounds like a lot of moving around—but not when it refers to aircraft structures. To jig is to hold firm while constructing, to keep the motion frozen while everything gets pinned together. This may be with a lowly clamp or Cleco holding together two pieces of metal while you work on them—or with the giant fixtures used to mate the wing and fuselage of the largest jets. In your case, of course, it consists of clamps, Clecos, screws, pipe, wood, plastic, just anything that will hold the structure you are working on in place and in proper alignment until you get it all pinned together.

Wings are the most critical because the depth of the airfoil is small compared with the cord and length and it is very flexible until most of the rivets are shot. See the manufacturer's maintenance manual, or the drawing in the case of a home-built, for detailed information about the rigging of the structures. A simple holding fixture can be made from a few two-by-fours. Just remember to use the tri-angle to get the rigidity. Support wings by the strut and butt fittings and at the tip. Six points will give you enough to hold the required rigging. Use metal angles with bolts or clamps. You will need a bubble protractor to check the rigging. The fuselage will require a cradle or two at mid-fuselage to fit the contour. Use a tripod for the aft section and a built-up frame for the fire wall. Just remember to give yourself enough room to work around the jig.

Once you've built a holding fixture, or jig, to do the job, you'll position and hold the parts at hard or secure points. Then drill a hole and insert a Cleco. Do the same at other points until you have the whole structure tied in tight.

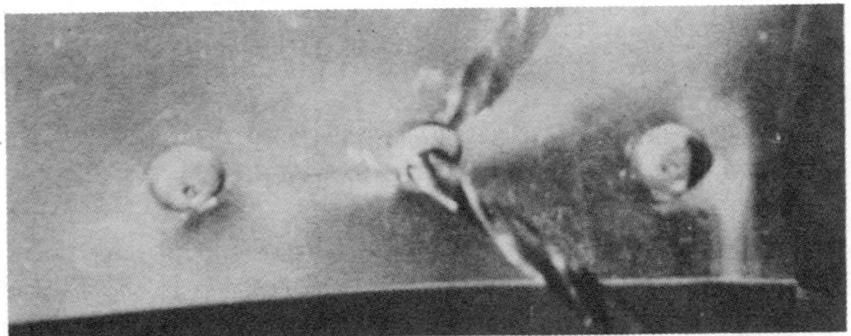

This very close shot shows how a drill is used to remove the head of a rivet during repair.

Now you can lay out the rivet patterns and bring all holes to the proper size for the rivets you're planning to use. Be generous with the Clecos if you want the structure to "stay put" and the rivets to fit with little or no reaming. Certain areas such as the leading edge skins and other sharply curved surfaces will require a progressive drilling and use of Clecos—a few on each rib, working away from the sharpest curve (such as the leading edge) along say two ribs at about one-third from each end of the leading edge. Once the skin is tight against these ribs, the rest can be drilled without the struggle you had with the first few.

One of the better ways (on repairs, usually the *only* one) is to locate the ribs and leading edge skins by back-drilling with an extension drill (usually a No. 40). This is a two-man operation: one man with the drill, the other guy with a board and the Clecos. At the start the ribs are easily moved. Pick up one at the forward, top or bottom of each rib, then tie to the tip or use a temporary diagonal brace to hold the position. Since the bottom or lower side is usually more flat, back-drill all the lower holes in the ribs, then remove the Clecos and clamp a straight angle to the edge and use a couple of angles to prop up the lower side. This will give easy access to the back-drilling of the top side. Work a few ribs as suggested before, then back-drill all the holes you can. After blowing away the chips, you're ready to thread rivets and shoot.

It hasn't been general practice to chromate the interior of most lightplane parts and structures—but it should be. Since air pollution seems to be ever-increasingly with us, the aircraft is affected. Many owners are encountering this problem at annual inspection time with ever-increasing expense. A good application of primer during a repair will greatly increase the life of the ship and save much in extra expense years later. It can be made a point of increased value at resale time, too.

The last major operation is riveting up all the parts—or is it riveting down? It all depends on the position of the structure and its design. You will just have to think your way through. Make a few dry runs with bar in hand. It will help, since on the close-up you can't see where the bar is in relation to the rivet. A dry run will help you to visualize the positioning of the bar when the skins are in place. It also helps to determine which rivet to shoot, and when, so that you'll be able to reach as many as possible. Blind rivets will finish the job, but are ten times more ex-

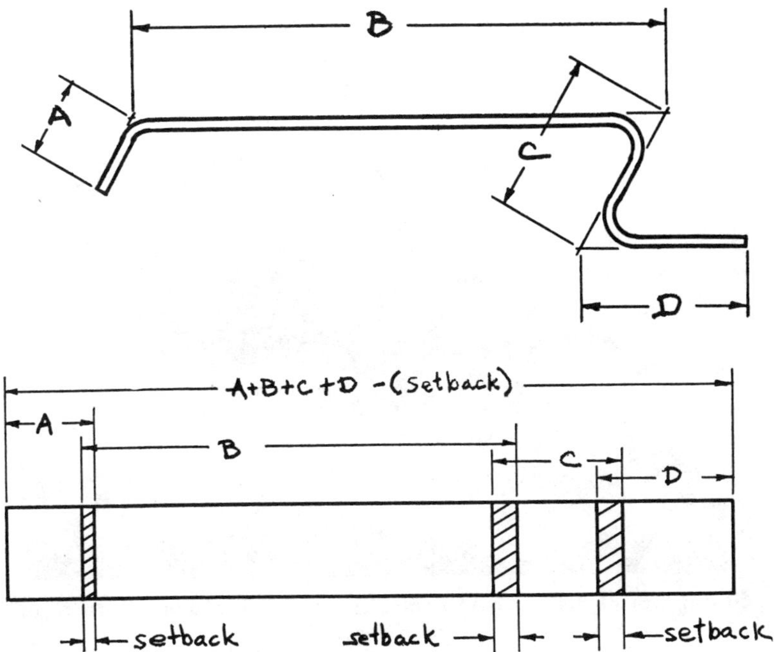

pensive than solid rivets. Usually the top surface is riveted first, then the bottom (in the case of wings and tail surfaces).

One rule which is a good one to remember and make a habit: *never* leave a bar inside—always bring it out with your hand. Then you'll never find yourself in the horrible predicament of having the job finished only to hear something rattling around inside.

Bucking rivets is an art, but fortunately it's one which can be acquired with a little experience and the use of your imagination. Always remember—some other guy riveted this structure and you're just as smart as he—aren't you?

Forming Metal

There are exactly three methods of forming sheet metal. You can:

    bend it
    stretch it, or
    shrink it.

No matter how complex the shape, every formed sheet metal object is made by a combination of these three operations. Consequently, if you are careful to learn all three of them, you will be able to make practically any part that is possible in sheet metal.

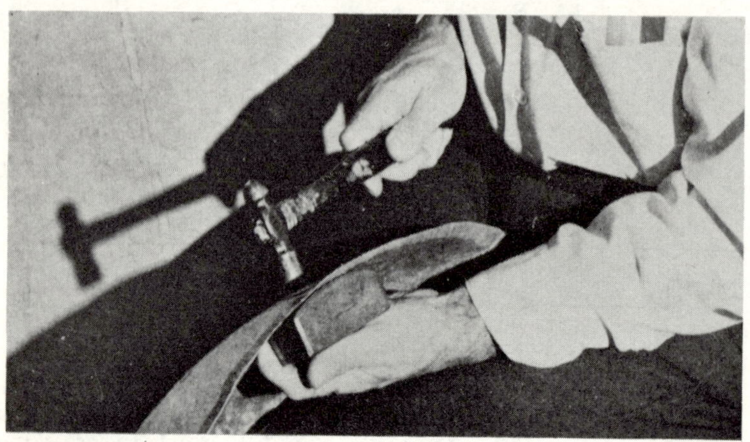

Curved face of dolly is held firmly against inside of part to stretch or raise sheet.

Bending is familiar to most of us, at least in principle. For aircraft work, accuracy is needed, so we must introduce the idea of bend allowance or set-back in the flat pattern dimensions. Metal cannot be bent to a sharp edge. Even if the inside were sharp, the outside would form a circular arc around it. In fact, very soft metals can be bent just this way. As a result of the curve, the length of material it takes to go around the bend is less than the sum of overall dimensions.

The difference in length is known as the set-back.* It can be calculated from the thickness, radius, and angle of bend. Notice in the illustration that the dimensions are given to an imaginary edge where the flat faces of a part meet. This is called the "mold line" and it is a conventional practice to give all sheet metal dimensions to it as a reference. When laying out the flat pattern of a bent sheet-metal part, you first lay out the mold lines of one face, then lay out the mold lines of the adjoining face, overlapping the first by the set-back distance as shown in accompanying example.

Hard materials such as those used in aircraft structures can

*See SETBACK chart on page 125.

be fractured by bending with too sharp a radius. There is a definite minimum bend radius (the inside radius) that will give satisfactory results for each material. The following are safe values to use:

- Non-structural aluminum alloys or annealed alloys — 2 times thickness

- Heat-treated aluminum alloys — 5 times thickness

- Low-carbon steel — 2 times thickness

- 4130 steel normalized — 4 times thickness

Condition of the edges and surfaces is important in forming sheet-metal parts. Nicks, scratches, and especially scribe marks cause localized high stresses during forming, and frequently cause the part to break or crack. Even if the part is formed successfully, these stress raisers often cause a fatigue crack in service. Therefore edges should be filed smooth, using strokes *parallel* to the edge. Scribe or punch marks should *never* be permitted in the actual part. Layout can be done with a soft pencil, or with a fine-tip marking pen.

A leaf brake is usually used for bending, but where this tool is not available a number of substitute arrangements can be used. In the brake, the material is clamped under the nose of the brake while the leaf swings up under the flange to bend it upward. Wood blocks can be used to clamp the material and provide the forming edge, while a mallet or another block can be used to drive the edge into position. All metals will spring back somewhat from the bent position, and clearance for this must be provided in any forming tools, about five degrees average for aluminum alloys.

Stretching sheet metal is just what the name suggests. You could do it be taking the ends of a piece and simply pulling until it gets longer. Some sheet-metal parts are formed in just that manner, by huge hydraulic stretch presses which simply pull the sheet over a form. Since we must usually be content with less equipment, we can resort to a much less elaborate device, a hammer. When a piece of metal is deformed, the volume remains about constant, so that it must get thinner as it gets longer. We can take advantage of this in reverse to stretch the metal. By making it thinner, we inherently make it longer. A sheet will spread out to cover a larger area when it is made thinner by hammering or rolling.

To stretch sheet metal, lay it against an anvil or surface plate, or hold a dolly against it, and strike it firmly with a flat-faced hammer. For most forming work, a small finishing hammer is best. It is important to remember that both surfaces touching

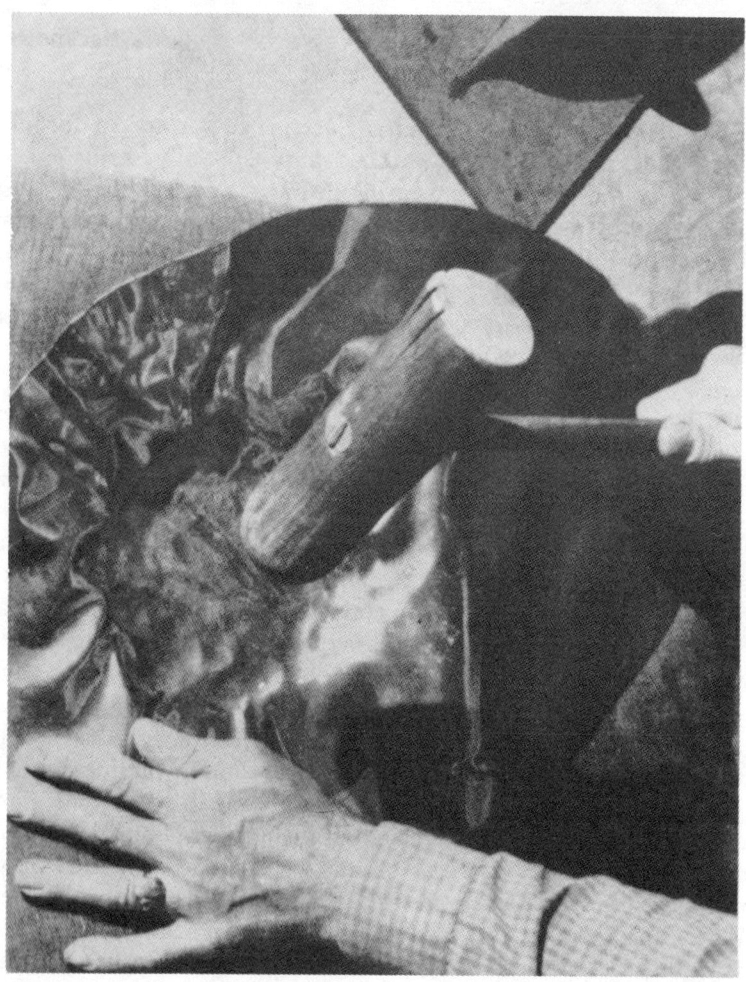

A. Stretching sheet into sandbag with wood mallet. Blunt end must be sanded smooth.

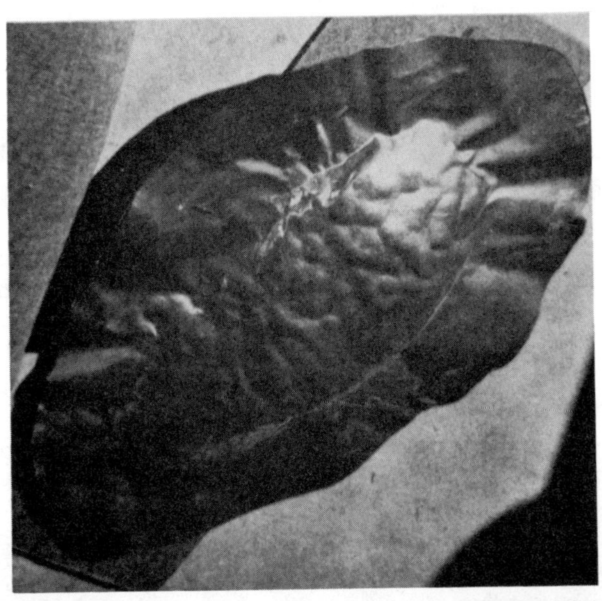

B. First half depth formed by stretching will be smoothed later with hammer and dolly. Outer portions will be formed by shrinking.

the sheet must be *polished*, for every scratch in the tool will be mirrored in the work every place you hit it. Remember too that you only stretch the metal by *squeezing* hard enough to reduce the thickness. Therefore, it must be in firm contact with the dolly or anvil. If you start with sufficient thickness, you can form a surprisingly deep contour by stretching alone.

Stretching is useful to straighten a flanged part which comes out curved where you want it straight. Long angles are usually curved or bowed because the bending process will actually stretch one flange a little. You can easily correct the bow by stretching the other flange to match, using a flat dolly or a surface plate.

The best method for forming a deep contour is to drive the sheet into a sandbag, using a fairly heavy mallet with a blunt end. The mallet can be made of hardwood such as oak or maple, and must be kept sanded smooth to avoid unwanted marks in the work. These are quite difficult to remove, and it is much less work to keep your tools in good shape. The mallet will form a series of dimples in the sheet, overlapping slightly to stretch a whole area uniformly. Very small parts can be formed with a ball peen hammer.

After the contour is rough-formed with the mallet and sandbag, it will have a pretty discouraging lumpy appearance. The contour is smoothed at this stage by a combination of further stretching, bending, and *shrinking*, so let's now take a look at the shrinking process and then come back to the rough part.

Just as you would expect, since shrink is the opposite of stretch, the sheet becomes thicker and covers less area when it shrinks. We can't pull the faces apart with a hammer to make the sheet thicker, but we can *drive* some of it *into a smaller area*. It's a little tricky, as there is danger of allowing a sharp fold to form. If that happens, you scrap the piece and start over, so pay close attention to the technique as we go through an example.

The easiest shrinking job is where a sharply contoured part has been stretched too far. In this case, a dolly is placed inside the part, bridging across the area to be shrunk so that it is supported only around the edge. The unsupported center can then be tapped in with a finishing hammer or even a flat mallet. Notice that both bending (around the edge) and shrinking occur. Don't hit very hard in this type of operation, because that might kink the metal. Instead, form a series of tiny flattened spots, first near the center, then spiraling outward until the rough shape is correct. Keep in mind the fact that a hammer works best by moving only a little material at a time. Control is much better with light blows. Another helpful trick is to use plenty of wrist action, and very little elbow motion, holding the hammer firmly at the thickest part of the handle.

A special tool is needed for the next method of shrinking. This

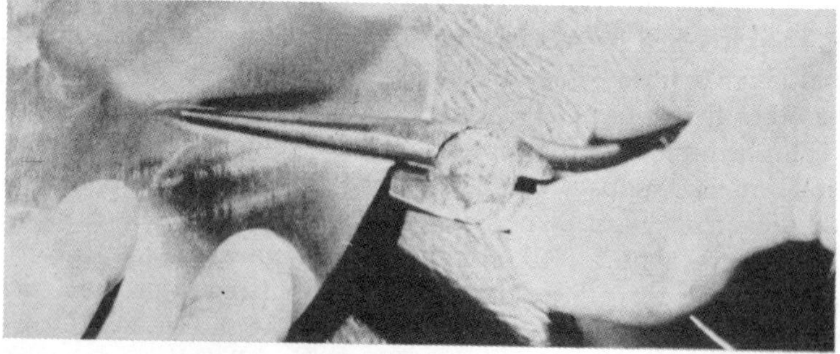

Shrinking pliers used to form conical wrinkle for smaller shrinks. Note rounded edges.

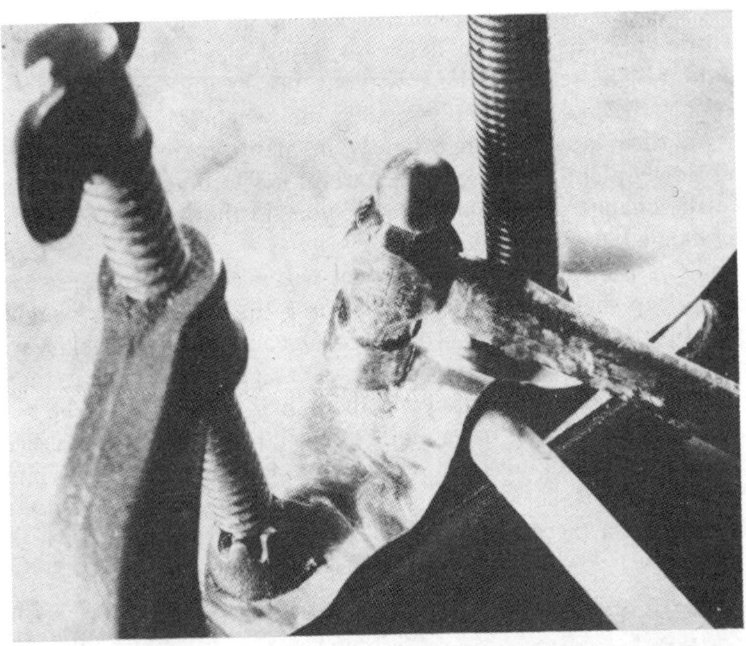

Forming small end of conical wrinkle down against plate to shrink material. Wood tool is used to control creases and feed material under hammer.

may be a pair of pliers similar to needle-nose pliers, but with no sharp edges or gripping pattern on the jaws. Another form often used is a simple "L" shaped steel bar with an extra cross bar, forming a slot into which the edge of a sheet can be inserted. Either of these tools can be used to bend the metal along the edge of a sheet into a conical wrinkle as shown.

This method is especially useful in straightening a bowed angle or an irregular channel such as a hand-formed rib. First, a wrinkle is formed at each point where shrinking is needed. Next, particularly if the wrinkles are fairly large, a tiny stiffening flange can be bent along the edge of each wrinkle. The end of a steel rod is a good anvil for this purpose. Finally, the edge of the sheet is laid down on a flat dolly or surface plate. Starting at the small end of the wrinkle, form the metal down flat against the dolly with the cross-peen end of the finishing hammer, and work out to the large end.

A flat part with a curved flange, such as a rib, may need just a little shrinking on the flange to adjust the bevel or smooth a contour. This can be done without taking up wrinkles, if you support the flat web firmly against the bench (clamp it if necessary), then tap the flange lightly in many, many places, working slowly along the length. Be careful *not* to hit so hard you can see the change after each blow. If you do that, you are bending the flange but not shrinking it.

The last shrinking technique you will need is the one used for large deep shapes like a nose cowl or a tip cap. To form such a part by stretching alone would require an excessive thickness to start, and would take a lot more effort (the easy way is tough enough). Therefore, we stretch about half the depth of the contour, and shrink the other half. On a large piece, that's a heck of a lot of shrinking, and we need a way to take large bites. Again, it will take a special tool, like nothing you've ever seen. This one is a piece of hardwood about an inch and a half in di-

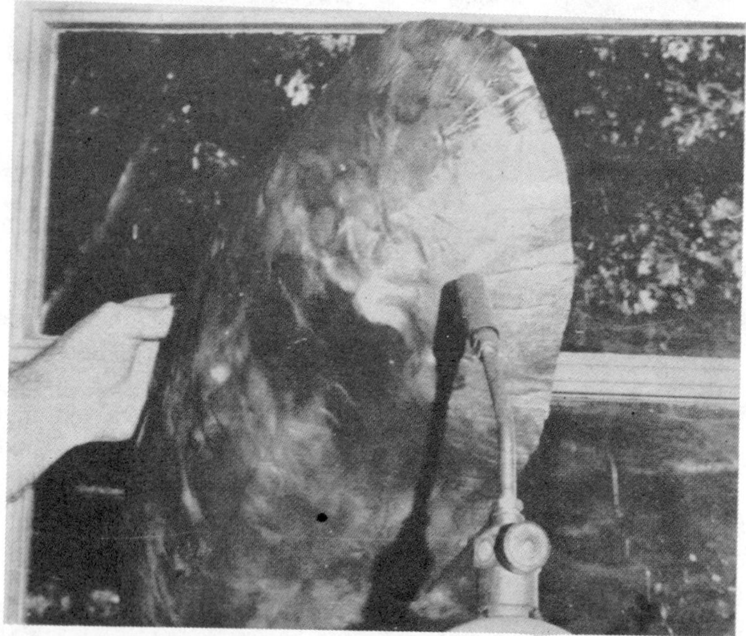

Light coating of soot from candle flame signals proper annealing temperature when it disappears in flame of torch. Torch must be kept in motion to avoid overheating spots.

ameter and two feet long. One end is shaped to a blunt point.

The procedure is similar to the one used for a flange, except that the wrinkles are huge this time, big enough to put the long tool nearly all the way inside the wrinkle. Instead of stiffening the edge, we stabilize the wrinkle by clamping the sheet on each side of it, working on a surface plate. Instead of a hammer, for this rugged job we use a heavy mallet to collapse the end of the wrinkle against the plate. By now, you have already realized that accuracy counts more than muscle in forming sheet metal. Even so, this is one forming job that takes plenty of muscle—you have to swing that mallet hard to make progress, but you'd better swing it accurately too, or you'll hardly make a dent in the job. This is where the long wood tool is priceless. You will find the sheet tends to break down into smaller wrinkles if you try to take too large a bit with the mallet. This will happen even when you're being especially careful.

Sample of formed sheet-metal fairing in place on "egg crate" of templates. Part was cut in half to show fit. Surface shows condition as hammered, after light sanding and hammer-smoothing, with one spot finish-sanded to illustrate typical appearances.

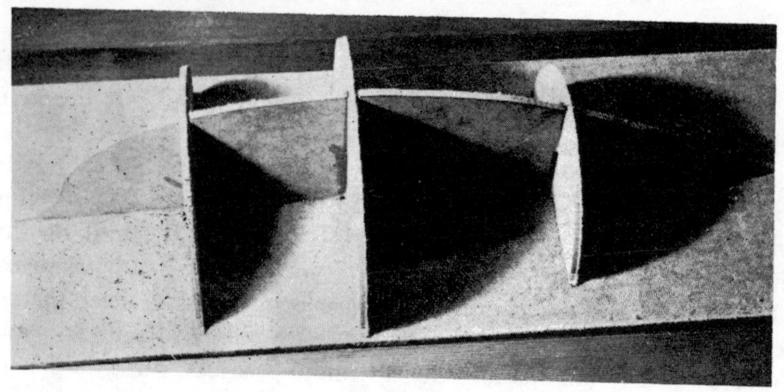

Detail of template "egg crate."

As soon as the small wrinkles form, *stop*. Then insert the long wood tool under the main wrinkle and work the tip in under the small ones to support the low area of the metal between small wrinkles. Resting the curved end of the tool on the plate, pry upward to lift the sheet and hold it while you flatten the small wrinkles. Use a smaller hammer for this if necessary. As you practice you will learn to detect the wrinkles as soon as they begin to form, and correct them instantly. That way, they aren't much trouble. Once a wrinkle forms, if you hit it again you will probably crease the metal sharply. This *always cracks* the sheet.

Although it *is* possible to repair a crack in a partly formed sheet, it is *not* easy. Frequently it just isn't practical, but if you must try, do this: First, trim a narrow strip off the edge of the same sheet, or another of the same alloy (three or four thicknesses wide). Next, using the strip as filler rod, weld the crack. Now you have a slug of cast material in place of the crack. By peening the weld, you convert it to nearly the same wrought (cold-worked) structure as the sheet. After filing off the excess material, you can proceed with forming, but don't be surprised if the crack reappears.

Occasionally, a shape is so complex it is almost impossible to form in one piece. If a single-piece finished part is really necessary, the same welding technique may be used to assemble formed pieces. These are carefully fitted so the edges butt exactly, and welded with continuous beads using the same alloy as filler. Only a short length of the seam should be welded at one time. Let this cool before proceeding, so that heat distortion is held to a minimum.

You now have the basic methods of forming sheet, but we haven't yet considered what happens to the metal as you form it. If you've been trying out the procedures described above, you have already noticed—it gets *harder*. It also becomes brittle, to the extent that you can hardly touch it with a hammer before it cracks. This condition is easily corrected by *annealing* the metal to soften it and restore the workable ductile quality. For aluminum alloys, heating to about 900°F and air cooling will restore the dead-soft temper, except the heat treatable alloys in the hard condition (T-3, T-4, T-6, T-8). For these alloys, this annealing schedule will remove most of the work hardening if you start with the 0 (soft) temper. Brass and copper are softened by heating to about 1200°F (bright-red heat) and quenching in water. Steel can be annealed by heating to the range 1000° to 1200°F and cooling slowly.

While all these metals can be annealed successfully with a torch, it is difficult to judge the temperature of aluminum alloys. The best way is to coat the metal with soot from a torch or candle flame, then heat just until the soot disappears. Further heating will almost certainly damage the material. The soot need not be applied heavily—a transparent coat will do nicely.

After forming the sheet to its final contours, there remains the problem of getting it really smooth. At this stage, it is likely to have hundreds of little flats, dents, and lumps. Some craftsmen prefer to *lightly* sand or file the surface at this point, primarily to make the flaws more visible. A piece of 1x2 pine with half a sheet of No. 60 open coat production paper (garnet) is just about right for this. Tacking the paper to the wood, use it as a file in long smooth strokes. As you stroke, rock the tool with a smooth motion, rolling it over the surface to make it follow a fair (smooth) curve. Take a series of parallel strokes in one direction, then choose another direction at least 60° away. The same technique is used later to finish the outside of the part, but for now just mark the surface. Now that you can see the irregular spots, here's how to smooth them up:

Reach inside the part and lightly "pick" the low spots outward with a ball peen. This isn't as difficult as it sounds. You will learn in a few minutes to hit accurately, while watching from the outside. Arrange the light in a glancing direction over the surface. After

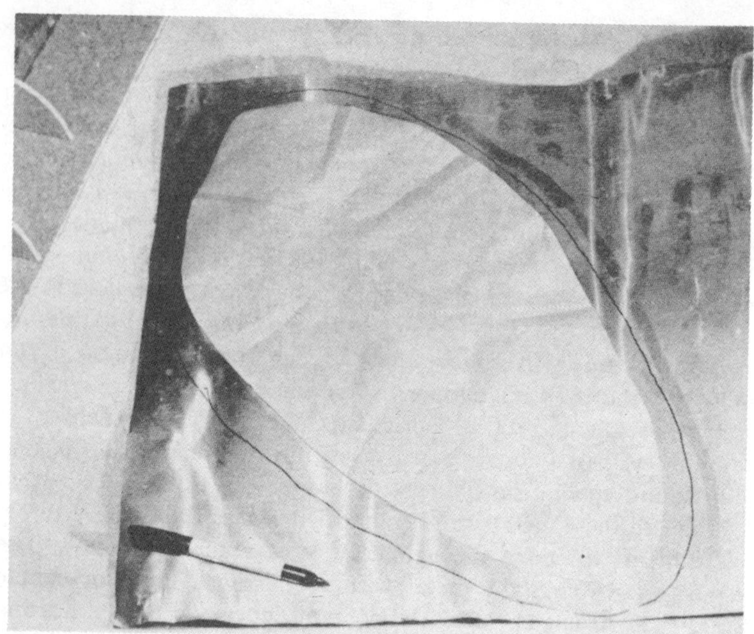

Paper pattern fitted to templates (note wrinkles) with trim line marked around it. Cut a generous pattern when part must be trimmed away as necessary. Pattern may be slightly repositioned on form.

Proper use of large tin snips to cut out pattern.

bringing the low spots out to the average contour, take a smoothly curved dolly of slightly sharper contour than the workpiece, hold it firmly against the inside surface. Now tap firmly with the finishing hammer on the outside, alternately shrinking the little high spots. and stretching or "raising" the low spots. You will quickly learn the difference in sound, as the dolly rings when you hit it squarely in a low spot where the metal is touching the dolly. Hitting a high spot where it bridges over the dolly, not touching, you get a dull sound. Be careful on the high spots not to hit too hard, because that drives the sheet against the dolly and stretches it instead of shrinking. The same technique is useful when there is a small area to shrink in a contour—just choose a dolly flat enough to bridge, and nudge the unsupported sheet down toward it.

As the work becomes smoother at this stage, you find it is sometimes easier to *feel* the rough spots or breaks in the contour than it is to see them. Running your hand lightly over the surface, you get a definite lumpy feeling where the contour is different from the rest. You can readily hit the spot from the underside with your hand there too.

The rest of the smoothing and finishing now is the simple part— hard and tedious work, but simple. This is the sanding and filing. The first part is done with a vixen file, using long flowing smooth strokes in two directions. Remember the object here is not to remove a lot of stock, but to just cut the high spots a little. Don't be reluctant to lay down the file and pick up the hammer again to touch up a spot. Don't bear down on that file, because every deep scratch or dig must be removed later with the garnet paper. Stop frequently to clear the chips out of the file—they cause most of the scratches.

As soon as the file seems to touch most of the surface, switch to garnet paper on a pine batten. There will still be a few spots to touch up with the hammer. Again, as the abrasive begins to hit most of the surface, go to a finer grade, finishing with about No. 240. The perfectionists will change to steel wool at this point. Others will use automotive primer-surfacer, at the expense of some extra weight. The most important thing in this final stage is to always use long smooth strokes to be sure of good fair contours, and apply them in *three* criss-cross directions, because the surface must be smooth in all directions to look smooth.

A true craftsman seen with his work. The late Sven Johnson, top and center, with the Lazor-Rautenstrauch racer. Nose cowl, cockpit fairings, and wheel pants were made entirely by hand hammering and power hammering. Lower photo shows a typical lightplane nose cowl formed by Mr. Johnson.

6. The Art of Welding

Welding is a *melting* process that allows the metal of two separate pieces to flow together and solidify as a single member. The nearby portions of the joined pieces form the container for the molten metal as the joint is being formed. Therefore, the whole process depends upon applying heat so intense and localized that only a small puddle of material is melted at one time. The puddle is formed and drawn along the joint by moving the heat source along slowly, so the advancing edge continuously melts a little new material as the trailing edge freezes at the same rate. Welders tend to move the heat in tiny steps, which gives the seams a characteristic appearance with a series of overlapping circular ridges.

Two things are most difficult for the beginner to learn. First, the weld must *penetrate,* that is, it must melt almost through the thickness of the material being joined, and that means through *both* parts. The back of a properly made joint has a slightly lumpy appearance where the material holding the puddle has sagged a little, because it was softened by the heat. The front shows a weld bead that is smoothly filleted into the unmelted base metal. A "cold" weld that does not penetrate into the base metal appears rounded up from the joined parts like a string of clay merely stuck in place. The back shows the original edges, not even softened by heat. Such a weld can often be broken by hand. The other difficult trick is to learn not to get the weld too hot. This results in the puddle falling through and melted edges drawing away from each other. In steel, excessive heat is signalled by the puddle exploding and popping molten metal on the tip of your torch. The correct technique for any weld requires a nice balance between cold welding and excessive heat. Luckily, it is quite easy to correct either one, by lifting the torch a little or moving it along a little faster if too hot, or the reverse if too cold.

A number of welding processes can be used successfully on aircraft structures. All of them are subject to the basic considerations outlined above. The differences are generally in the method of heating. For steel, there are three processes of interest, oxy-acetylene, electric arc, and heliarc. Although spotwelding is also acceptable, it is a machine process requiring very elaborate equipment, and is not considered for the amateur.

Oxy-acetylene is the most common technique, using a torch that mixes oxygen and acetylene from separate tanks. When the torch is properly adjusted, it will produce a long flame with a small blue-white inner cone. This cone is the intense heat source. Holding the torch so the flame blows forward in the direction of progress along the joint, you can preheat the work as you go. The actual welding heat is taken from the side of the cone. A right-handed welder thus welds from right to left. This is called the "forehand" technique. Since it permits a good view of the work, it is easier than some others to learn. As for any joining process, the material to be welded must be thoroughly cleaned. Steel can be cleaned with a steel wire brush (other materials leave deposits that interfere with welding), but aluminum usually requires chemical cleaning such as caustic etch. Sheet metal joints in aluminum can be cleaned by scraping with a broad sharp wood chisel to remove the surface layer of oxidized metal, if carefully degreased first. A solvent such as thinner will remove greases and oils.

Dark neutral-colored goggles are best for welding steel. On aluminum, however, many of the fluxes emit a brilliant orange flame that obscures the work. For this, blue goggles are more suitable.

Filler rods for steel should be plain mild steel, unless the parts are heat treated after welding. In that case, a special grade of rod must be used for each base material, and must be specified by the designer. Aluminum parts are usually welded with the "silicon" rod, 4043 alloy, which gives the best all around results. It is often satisfactory to use a strip of the base metal as a filler rod, although some alloys like 6061 are difficult to handle with it. Arc welding electrodes of the same materials are used.

Filler should be used sparingly, sometimes only to control movement of the puddle. Particularly going up a vertical seam, the rod can be used to draw the puddle along by means of surface tension in the molten material. Care is necessary to avoid cold welds when using the rod in this fashion. If an excessive amount of filler is needed, it probably means the parts were not properly fitted before welding, and large gaps are being filled. This results in a weak joint, because the strength of weld material is usually much less than that of the parent metal.

Flux is not used for gas welding steel, so that an oxide scale forms on the surfaces, which must be removed by wire brushing or light sandblasting before any finish is applied. Flux coated electrodes are used for arc welding, causing a slag to form on the parts. This can be removed in the same manner, or with a small chipping hammer. Heliarc welding is shielded by inert helium, so that no oxides form, and no cleaning is required after welding. Fluxes used for aluminum welding usually can be removed by hot water rinsing.

Additional information on welding materials and techniques can be found in the instruction manuals furnished with the equipment being used, and in the manuals published by the material manufacturers. The material producers' manuals can usually be obtained free of charge through their local sales offices. All major steel and aluminum makers provide such manuals.

Detailed instructions and limitations for repairs on welded structures are published in Advisory Circular 43.13-1 and these should be studied carefully in preparation for any repair. A few general cautions are:

- never weld over existing weld
- never weld heat-treated parts
- always be sure of the material before attempting to weld it
- always be sure the parts are well supported before welding

Dimensional control of welded parts and assemblies is important and difficult enough to warrant a separate discussion entirely apart from the welding techniques.

Because welding is a melting process, the parts being joined get really hot, even some distance from the weld itself. All materials change their size with changing temperature, expanding usually as the temperature increases. Steel melts around 2800° F, so that temperatures approach 3000° at the weld. Aluminum melts at about 900°, but it is such a good conductor, and expands so much more per degree, that the overall result is much the same in both materials.

As the weld is being formed, the material is actually molten right at the joint, and it is so hot nearby that it is very soft. Therefore, the parts cannot support themselves during welding operations. Some kind of fixtures must be used to support the parts, even if they are improvised from C-clamps and two-by-fours. The trick is to provide enough support of the right kind, but *not restrain expansion and contraction* due to temperature changes. Very high stresses can be developed in the parts if expansion is restrained, and this may cause buckles, thinned out sections, or harmful strain-hardening that can make parts fail at much less than their design loads.

Even the exact sequence of weld can seriously affect the condition and dimensional accuracy of the parts. One of the most useful tricks is to make a series of tack welds, along the length of a joint, allowing the parts to cool after each tack. Especially in sheet and plate joints, this avoids a lot of edge movement that can open up large gaps and make life difficult for the welder. This practice is acceptable despite the general ban against welding over existing welds, which refers to complete joints. Permitting the parts to cool after welding part of a joint is nearly always a good idea, because it holds thermal expansion and movement to the absolute minimum. It is most helpful on the more complex assemblies, and it should *always* be done where the shrinkage of one joint cooling would pull on another joint.

The sequence is especially important for large welded structures, such as a fuselage truss. Generally, the best practice on these is to weld each cluster complete, *and normalize it,* before going on to the next. Each bulkhead or frame is welded complete before the next. Naturally, some judgment is necessary here, as you may have two clusters so close together that heating one to welding or normalizing temperature will heat the other enough to affect its condition. In such a case, of course, the two should be heated together for normalizing after the welds are finished. If the parts get hot enough to form a blue oxide film (similar to gunmetal blue) the temperature is over 600°F, and may affect the physical properties of the metal.

You can see how powerful the thermal expansion is by heating just one side of a tube with a welding torch. The tube will bow away from the heat, and you can move the end of a fairly long piece several feet by heating near the support.

Assembly of a large structure should never be attempted without a jig. The temptation is quite strong to take liberties, especially if you are making only one assembly. However, the accuracy of dimensions simply cannot be guaranteed without a pretty husky jig, and even with it there is some doubt. Welded fuselages in production, for example, rarely come out the same from one to the next until a number have been made, and the best sequence of joints has been established. The jig should be heavier stuff than the structure, and should hold each tube so it can slide lengthwise. A good support is a piece of angle iron to nest the tube, with a band or even a twist of wire to hold the tube against the angle.

Longerons or other members running the whole length of an assembly should be cut substantially longer than the assembly will be. These members will shrink as each joint along the way cools, often a sixteenth or more for each joint. That is the reason it pays to do all the joints at each frame in one series before going on to the next frame. It doesn't make much difference which end is done first, but often the forward end of a fuselage mates with heavy fittings on wing or engine mount, and the fit will be less affected if that end is done first. You may find the uneven strains cause the assembly to bow or warp as you proceed around a bulkhead. This can be alleviated if you have someone heat the opposite longeron as you weld, to balance the strains.

One thing to avoid like the plague is tacking a large structure like a fuselage at all joints before welding. If the tackwelds hold, which isn't likely, they are sure to cause distortion. Tacking should be used only on small assemblies like fittings, or where edges must be precisely fitted, such as the seams in a multipiece formed sheet-metal part or a tank seam.

Summing up, the three methods of dimensional control are:

- sequence
- cooling the assembly between welds, and
- adequate jig support

Remember that welded assemblies are simply not like bolted and riveted assemblies in stability. Even after completion, they do change a little with time, especially in the presence of vibratory loads big enough to affect the condition of the materials. If you practice carefully the three methods of control, however, you can achieve a thoroughly practical result with sufficient accuracy to fit up with the rest of an airplane.

7. Easing Into Reinforced Plastics

Reinforced plastic materials are among the most useful and convenient for the amateur builder. They offer some of the best physical properties, take very simple tooling, permit any shape, and are not more expensive than other materials to any important extent. However, there are some serious disadvantages too. The strength of RP materials depends completely on the way you do the fabrication. Some materials are not entirely compatible with others you might wish to use in the same structure or assembly. Some require very elaborate equipment and processing. Therefore, it is necessary to select the materials very carefully to be sure of satisfactory results in the final product. Don't be discouraged about all the notes of caution. The authors believe the fiberglass reinforced plastics are the very best aircraft materials available today, and will be the most popular in the future. If you stick to the recipe, you can be assured of good results. The Navy recently removed a large fiberglass fairing from a submarine conning tower . . . in near-perfect condition—after *eleven years* of submarine service. Steel and aluminum units had previously given up after a few months each.

There are two groups of plastics of interest for aircraft structures, the polyesters, and the epoxies. Both include numbers of different materials that have useful properties and require different processes. Both have been widely used with great success in aircraft.

The polyesters are the older materials, and are less expensive generally than the epoxies. Structural qualities are about equal in the two families, so it is perfectly legitimate to select on some other basis, provided you stay within the sub-families that are known to be satisfactory in strength. The points to be checked are:

- strength
- cure temperatures
- cure pressures
- availability of material and technical data
- cost
- compatibility with your adhesives
- resistance to ultraviolet light (sun)
- maximum service temperature

Most of the major chemical manufacturers in this country have developed their own systems of one or both resin types. Each producer will be glad to furnish detailed technical information on his products and help you choose the ones suited to your needs. Room temperature curing in air makes it possible to work with the simplest possible tools, without vacuum bags or ovens. Resins which can be cured in this manner can be processed also in the more complicated ways, and will have better strength as a result, but you can always get by without much equipment, if you must, with these materials.

Polyesters which air-cure usually have paraffin in them to exclude air from the surface. This affects their ability to bond with other materials, and limits the choice of adhesives to those in which the paraffin is harmlessly soluble, such as polyester resins.

Polyesters which do not air-cure require a cover, such as a sheet of PVA film, to prevent contact with air, unless the mold covers both sides of the laminate. These are usually vacuum-bag molded, and usually can be bonded with any general purpose structural adhesive.

Epoxy resins can be fabricated by the same methods generally, and will bond satisfactorily with any structural adhesive. Most of the room temperature curing epoxies will also air-cure without special additives.

Reinforcing materials can be obtained in a wide variety of woven and knitted fabrics, fiber mats, and chopped fiber. The principal caution on these is that there are many commercial reinforcing products made for easy draping on complex forms or to ensure easy wetting, which do not provide a high strength in the finished part. The best way to avoid problems here is to use only the materials which are qualified under the Military Specifications. MIL-C-9084 is the main specification governing the quality of the reinforcement. FAA has published a guide to the application of fiberglass laminates in civil aircraft, Advisory Circular 20-21, *Application of Glass Fiber Laminates in Aircraft*. Copies may be obtained from the Government Printing Office in Washington, D.C.

Finish on the reinforcement has a powerful influence on strength of the laminate, since it controls the actual mating surface between the resin and the glass. Several modern finishes give excellent results, and the supplier will be glad to furnish information on this.

Most important is to choose a family of materials that gives useful results *when prepared by methods you can use in your own project.* Remember the properties of your material will vary over a wide range, according the conditions of your particular process.

Any compound shape made of metal requires skill, experience and tools. However, the same parts can easily be duplicated in RP. Cowlings, light or beacon housings, fairings, scoops, wing tips, spinners—all can be made easily and inexpensively. In fact, you'll find more and more RP being used on current models.

Since you are most likely interested in one-of-a-kind parts for your ship, we'll go over the easiest way to do this. You will need a model or a form of the part. Make one of wood, clay, plaster, papier-maché, or perhaps a metal part from another ship that will suit your purpose. The exterior shape is what you want so you'll have to make a female mold of the part. This, too, can be made of almost any material which will maintain the part's shape for as long as you'll need it.

If you expect to use the mold more than once you'll have to make it of materials that will hold up. Plaster or RP work quite well. Plaster is very rigid but chips and cracks easily. RP is preferred since it can be made with a thin flexible laminate which will hold the shape of the form; it can be reinforced and it is light. You'll be able to lay-up more than one part, make small changes, cut here or add there, until you get just what you want. Note in picture how plywood is used to support the RP. It's attached to the mold with RP strips.

You'll have to spend some time grinding, sanding and filing to get a smooth surface. Realize that the smoothness of the mold surface will determine how the part will turn out. Rough mold, rough part. It won't matter for one part since this can be reworked to your liking. But with more than a few parts it will pay you to take a few pains with both the form and the mold.

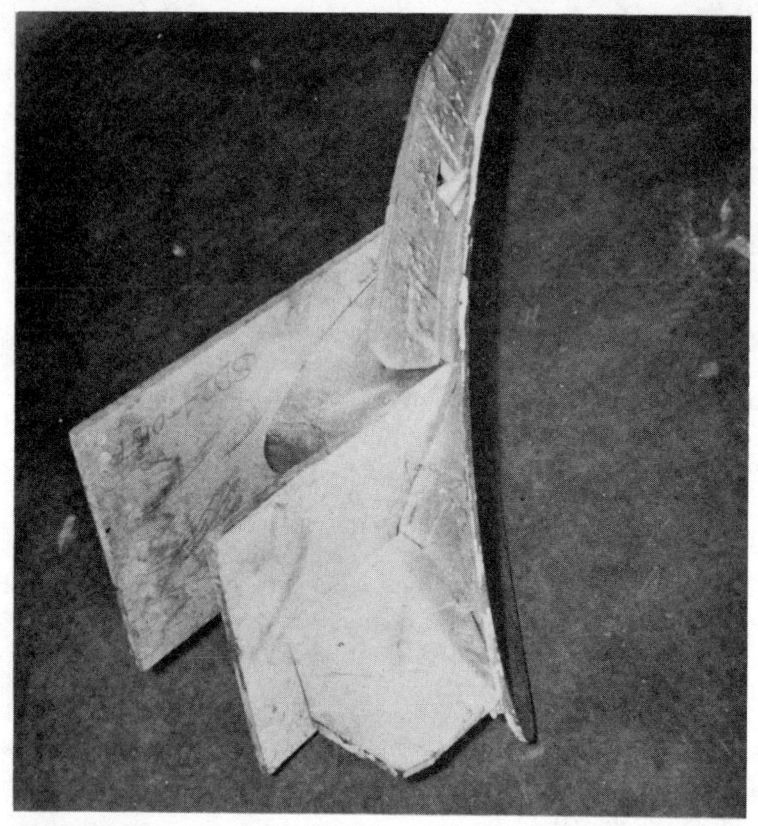

This fiberglass mold is supported by roughly cut plywood secured to the mold with tabs of fiberglass saturated with resin.

If you are interested in quality, even on just this new part, then you'll want to use a Gel coat. This is a type of resin with a formulation for flexibility and it is usually sprayed on the mold first, to reduce air bubbles or voids in the surface. It's only a few thousandths of an inch thick but it will give your mold and part a smooth, void-free surface. The Gel coat may have color added either as a back-up for painting or to retain a desired color without painting. After the Gel coat has cured, a lay-up of RP is made to desired thickness and supported.

You will need a few tools, some equipment and a place to work which has some adequate ventilation. Some of the materials are quite volatile, so smoking should be banned and a fire extinguisher should be handy.

Temperature is important: usually not below 60°F. High temperature is a problem only in that you'll have to work·so fast that only small parts can be made. Air movement over a mold should be kept to a minimum. It will affect the Gel and cure-time cycles and will tend to dry out the resin surface. This affects viscosity and causes dragging of the surface while you are trying to work the resin into the fiberglass.

You'll need tools and equipment such as: saw, files, razor knife, a sander, drill, cans of unwaxed paper buckets, brushes, scissors, clamps, tongue depressors, small paint roller, thermometer, scraper, 10 cc measure, small scale up to 10 lbs., bundle of rags or wipers. And for materials: resins, MEK-peroxide (a catalyst), acetone, sandpaper (120-320-400-500), coarse and fine compound PVA, wax, fiberglass cloth and mat.

It is most important to obtain a manufacturer's specification sheet on the resins you are going to use—*then follow it*. Most resins require the addition of one or two elements for a reaction to take place and the resin to become rigid. The spec sheet tells you what is to be added, how much, by weight, and how long you'll have to work with the resin (its "pot life") before Gel or a semi-rigid condition starts. Once Gel starts you won't be able to work the resin any longer except to trim around the edges of the mold.

Gel is also accompanied by heat—the higher the percentage of catalysis, the higher the temperature and shorter pot life. A thicker laminate will also generate more heat.

You'll note the spec sheet will give you a chart showing the relationship of percent of catalyst, temperature and pot life. You'll be able to control the pot life with percent of catalyst. It's a good idea to set up a small quantity of the resin in a cup and add a controlled percentage of catalyst. Check the time to Gel. If you feel it is too short, then cut the percentage until you get the pot life you will need to complete the lay-up. Sometimes you'll find some difference in Gel-time because of the age of the resin or catalyst. Even humidity can have an effect. These tests will tell you what to expect right now.

Before you start, get everything set up so that once you catalyze the resin you can follow through without interruption. The mold or form should be well waxed, rubbed down, and then sprayed with PVA and allowed to dry. If a Gel coat is to be used it must be applied and allowed to cure before lamination. Cut oversize pieces of all cloth and mat you intend to use ino this lay-up. Position your brushes, can of acetone, scissors, roller, sticks, etc., within easy reach.

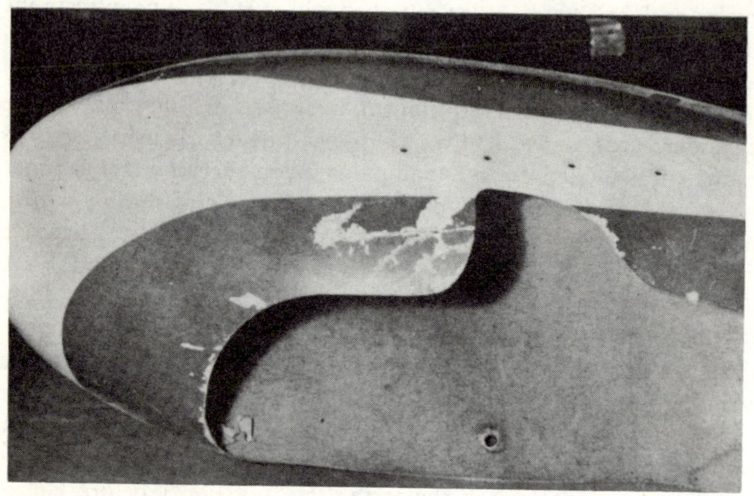

A typical damaged fiberglass wheel fairing.

Now weigh out resin and measure the catalyst to be used. All set? Mix and stir thoroughly. Brush a coat of resin over the entire mold or form, then lay on the fiberglass cloth and/or mat. Add more resin by dabbing with the brush. Brushing will pull the cloth or mat. Start in the middle and work to the edges. Now use the roller. Its function is to press the cloth or mat firmly to the mold and bring the air bubbles to the surface. You can do this with the brush but it takes much longer. Now add mat and/or cloth layers, using just enough resin to wet the fiberglass until you have the desired thickness. Certain areas, such as attach points, may require the addition of fiberglass strips to build up a thicker edge for stiffness—or a ready-made fiberglass or metal stiffener—or metal inserts at attach points. Don't forget to clean the brush, rollers, etc., before the Gel. Use acetone for cleaning.

On large parts such as cowlings it may be necessary to make the lay-up in two or more stages, waiting for a hard cure and cool-down of laminate before starting another lay-up. You will just have to play it by eye and experience.

Just after a Gel and before the hard cure is a good time to do any trimming—around the edges or the openings that have been built in the mold. Use a razor knife. You'll find the cutting is very easy and it will save you some hard work after the hard cure.

As a general rule, leave the part in the mold at least until the cure is complete and the heat has dissipated. The part will continue to cure for another 48 hours. Overnight is enough. To remove the part from the mold, use the tongue depressors. They're soft and flexible and won't scratch the mold or the part. Start around the edges and work the sticks between the mold and part, progressing around the edge and deeper and deeper in. Then apply a steady, light pressure, pulling on the part. You'll hear it breaking away from the mold. Sometimes air pressure can be used to advantage to help the breakout.

Once out, the PVA film can be removed with water—and wax with acetone. The part is now ready for trimming and fitting.

Unless you've checked the fit on the original form, now is the time to see how the part fits on the aircraft. If you find the part it just slightly oversize, all you need is a file or sandpaper. But if much trimming is required, it might be necessary to make a stiff paper template for a rough fit—then pencil-line the outline on the part. Use a hacksaw or bandsaw, then hand file or sand to the desired fit. Once fitted, pencil mark the attach points or even drill undersize holes and use small screws or Clecos.

RP is not as hard as metal, nor as strong. It's more like wood, in that it won't take high bearing loads. Holes should have an edge distance of 5 or 6 times the diameter of the hole. Washer head screws should be used or a washer with a screw. If anchor nuts are used they should be attached with wide head rivets. Rubber bushings with large diameter washers may be used where vibration is present, for example engine cowling and wheel fairings. A large diameter metal patch can be riveted (again, with soft rivets) directly to the RP part.

These are only suggestions. You'll work out the best method for your project. One important point to remember: don't pull up too hard on screws or bolts. Just make them firm but tight.

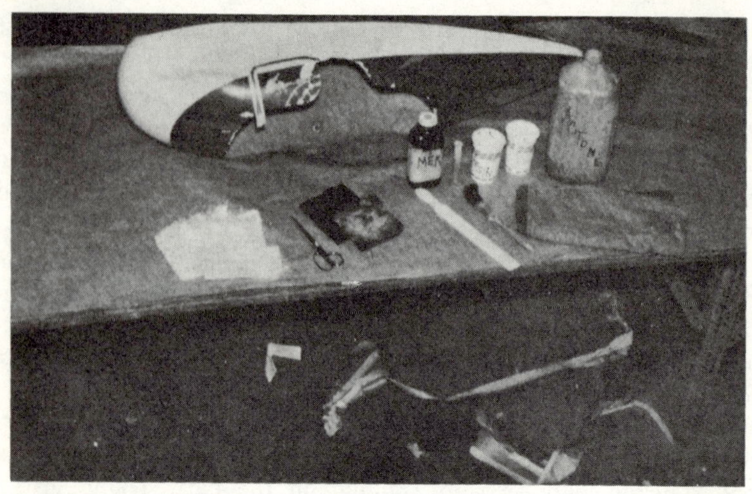

Here are all the materials you'll need to effect a repair to the wheel fairing.

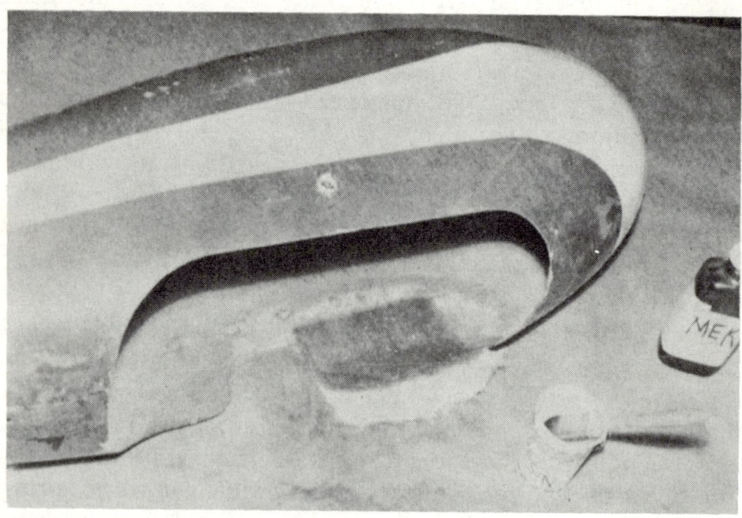

After a good cleaning with acetone a piece of fiberglass is laid on the inside and saturated with resin catalyzed with MEK. Within a few minutes it'll set up enough to wet trim. In a few hours it'll be as hard as the original.

Wing tips and wheel fairings and even cowlings seem to bump into things from time to time. If they are not too badly damaged, repairs can be made more cheaply than replacing the part. As a general rule, try to make most of the repair on the inside with only a single laminate outside. This way you will best retain the original shape. If the broken parts are still at hand, try to piece them together in position and support with masking tape, screws . . . any way to maintain the shape . . . from the outside.

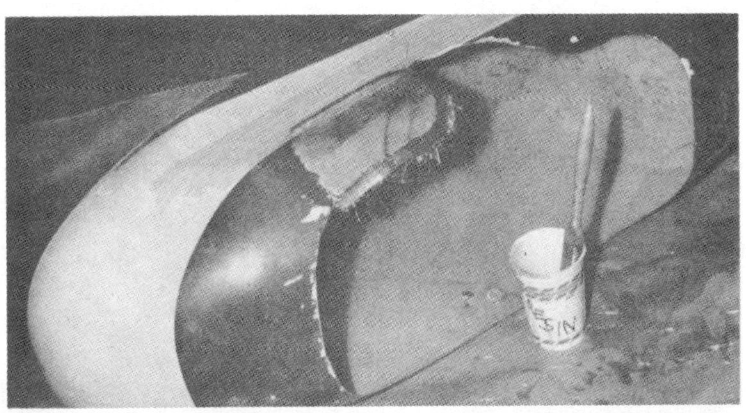

Another layer of fiberglass and resin is applied to the outside surface which, after a hard cure, will be ready to trim, sand, prime and paint.

If some pieces are missing, you will have to make a mold of some sort . . . just so it gives the approximate shape . . . from the outside if possible. Clean up the inner surface with a grease solvent, then acetone. With sandpaper or a rotary sanding disc, remove paint and sand to the first layer of fiberglass. Allow two to four inches overlap beyond all cracks or breaks in the laminate. Cut the fiberglass mat and cloth to the shape of the repair. Remember to use enough material to double the original thickness.

Now get all the equipment and materials you'll need for the job ready and laid out. You'll proceed as described earlier for a lay-up. Once cured, remove the temporary mold and/or tape from the outer surface. Prepare and fabricate the outer surface the same as before . . . except use only a ply or two. Fill up dents and depressions, of course, and allow for sanding to shape. Once a hard cure has been obtained you can sand to shape, fill voids, sand again, attach hardware, prime, and paint. It'll be hard to tell it's been damaged! Cracks in cowling can be repaired in a similar manner.

Preparation for painting is the real answer to getting a good finish. First remove all traces of mold release wax and old paint. Use solvent but *not* paint remover. (There is an interaction which softens the resins.) You will have to sand off the old paint down to the RP. Scratches or voids are filled with a resin-type body filler then sanded smooth when hard. Since RP is in general use, the paint companies have developed primers especially for it. Check with the auto supply store where you buy your paint.

8. Wood Structures for Aircraft

Wood is probably the oldest structural material used by man. Still useful today, it has served well in aircraft construction for many years, and has even been reported to have gone into space on Russian satellites. One of the most highly developed uses of wood in aircraft was in the famous *Mosquito* bomber of World War II. Most of this aircraft was made up of wood sandwich panels, a lightweight balsa core with strong hardwood faces.

As you might expect, the properties of wood differ widely, even for a given type. Consequently, it is necessary to select the material carefully to obtain the best strength. Of the dozens of woods available, only a handful are considered primary aircraft materials. Sitka spruce is the principal choice for solid members, such as wing spars. For thin panels, birch and mahogany are favored in the form of plywood.

Because other materials have surpassed wood in popularity, there is little recent published information. Even the Forest Products Laboratory* has concentrated on improved wood products and fiberglass the last few years. During the 1940s, an excellent and comprehensive manual was prepared and published as ANC-18, *Design of Wood Aircraft Structures*, available from the Government Printing Office in Washington, D.C. For the serious home-builder, this publication is a must, as it includes both the physical properties of the species and forms of wood available, and also the most successful design and construction practices to follow.

Currently applicable military specifications should be used as a guide for the purchase of any aircraft wood or plywood. While commercial products are often of very good quality, there is no way

---

*U. S. Department of Agriculture, Madison, Wisconsin.

of knowing exactly what they are, nor that the quality is uniform from one piece or batch to the next.

Adhesives for use in wood aircraft structures must be moisture-resistant, and must produce bonds that are stronger than the wood being joined. Many good synthetic resin glues are available which are entirely satisfactory. Again, the current military specifications should be used as a guide.

While the supplier of materials can provide data on the products that meet specification requirements, you can find a good deal of helpful information and a list of materials in Civil Aeronautics Manual 18, Appendix B. This manual also includes very explicit information on repair practices for wood aircraft, including the approved substitutes for various species. Another Army-Navy-Commerce bulletin, ANC-19, *Wood Aircraft Inspection and Fabrication*, includes detailed instructions on the actual techniques to be used. This is also available from the Government Printing Office. AC 43. 13-1 supercedes CAM 18, and includes much of the same information.

Making parts for wood aircraft is comparatively simple, based generally on common good-quality woodworking practices. Special care is necessary, however, to make sure the wood is properly conditioned before use. Material purchased under government specifications is stabilized at 15% moisture content because this is about the final average for service in the continental U. S. Parts made from material much different from this content are likely to swell or shrink enough to cause splitting or glue joint failures. Aircraft structures usually have a number of metal fittings, bolts, bushings, etc. in the wood or fastened to it. These resist dimensional changes, causing the trouble.

Protective finishes do *not* prevent changes in the moisture content. They do slow down the process, but don't stop it. Therefore, an excessively dry or moist workroom is to be avoided if you expect good results. That means the average heated building is definitely not suitable in the winter, unless the humidity is controlled.

Actual fabrication is essentially the same as most good furniture and cabinet work, using the same tools and equipment. There are some exceptions. For example, sanding is used very little on the detail parts. Faces to be glued should *never* be sanded, because that causes a definite loss of strength. The surface should be planed or scraped to final size and smoothness in preparation for gluing.

Other practices not found in other types of woodworking include the use of finer saws for most cutting, more frequent use of the scraper in finish cuts, and greater care to ensure straightness of long pieces. The fine-tooth saw is useful in reducing the amount of work to obtain the final smooth surface, while maintaining dimensional accuracy. This is necessary because rough surfaces reduce the strength. Scrapers are widely used instead of sanding, especially where a contour is required. The scraper blade is easily made from any fairly hard steel sheet (scraps of 4130 are fine) around .065. The working edge is filed square or slightly bevelled, and in use it is drawn along the work smoothly with both hands. A draw knife is often used for the heavier cutting just before the scraper. These are especially useful on aerodynamic surfaces, such as the solid leading edge of a plywood covered wing or tail, where the contour is too sharp for bending plywood. Straightness in the long pieces is more critical in the aircraft work, because there usually isn't as much other material to force it into line, and the grain slope that causes it to bow in the first place can't be tolerated.

Band saw, table saw, cross-cut handsaw, planer, and large woodworking clamps are the mainstays in any aircraft wood shop. Many other tools are useful too, but these are the ones you can scarcely do without.

Detail parts should be given a protective finish as soon as they are completed, except faces that are to be glued. This slows down the exchange of moisture with the air, so that short term highs and lows in humidity don't have too much effect.

The scarfed ends of pieces to be glued and doubler plates are cut at very long slopes. This is very awkward around the shop, but it is also vital in developing the full strength of a structure. Joints with less than a 15- or 20-to-1 slope will not even come close to the strength of the basic members.

In order to meet your finished dimensions with the least handwork, you should stick to the finer tooth blades in both table saw and bandsaw for the final sizing cuts. This means you will be changing blades fairly often, and it will pay to lay out the work in batches, so as to use one blade for as long as possible at one time.

Wood, like metal, is notch-sensitive. This means any sharp inside corner or scratch can reduce the effective strength of a part.

The material should be treated with the same respect as smooth finished metal. Grain direction is extremely important, too, in controlling the strength of wood parts. Strength can vary as much as fifty percent with the grain or across it. Detail parts should, therefore, be made with great care to put the grain direction where the designer specified it.

Many of the smaller parts in wood aircraft are all alike. One good example is the glue block, a simple triangular cross section strip. Lengths differ, but this piece is used wherever two parts join at right angles, to provide adequate glue area. Rib capstrips and rib truss members are usually of the same cross section also. Any parts of this kind should be made up all at one time and stock lengths put in storage until needed. A little planning on such parts will save a great deal of time by avoiding unnecessary repeated setups. Often a simple jig or cutting guide clamped on the table of a saw will speed up the cutting of standard lengths from the long stock.

Marking the part numbers carefully on the wood is another trick that will save time. A felt tip marking pen can be used for this purpose. Separate tags often become detached.

Bending

Discussion until now has been centered on the fabrication of parts that can be cut to final shape. Although some require hand shaping with planer or draw knife, the fabrication is essentially a cutting process. Many aircraft parts, however, require bending either a strip of solid wood or a sheet of plywood. The technique for bending is compartively simple, but must be done very carefully to avoid breaking the part.

As its moisture content is increased, and as the temperature increases, wood becomes quite plastic. In this condition, it can be formed over comparatively small radii—in the order of thirty times the thickness for plywood thoroughly soaked at a temperature near boiling. Best results are obtained if the wood can be steamed in a closed container. With more care, however, it can be handled almost as well using cloth wrappings heavily soaked with boiling water.

If a large or thick piece must be bent over too small a radius, the part can be built up of several thinner pieces by laminating. When plies are correctly laminated with no joints or discontinuities in the assembly, the laminated part is equal in strength to a solid piece of the same material. It is important to realize that bending and laminating cannot be done at the same time, since excess water may affect the glue performance. Bent parts should be held to the form with clamps as much as possible. If additional holding is necessary, a limited number of nails can be used. Nails should be driven through a wood batten or heavy cloth tape such as cotton rib-stich reinforcing tape. This provides better clamping action without damage to the parts, and enables you to remove the nails after the parts have set in the desired shape. Only small nails should be used for this purpose, and they should be smooth, not serrated, to facilitate removal.

Assembly methods for wood aircraft are limited. Glue, wood screws, and bolts are satisfactory in properly designed joints. Nails are not suitable. Various patented or proprietary fasteners can be obtained for wood structures, but most of these are completely unsuitable for aircraft because they reduce the strength of the basic members being joined. There may be some of suitable design, but there are no established data on which FAA approval might be based. The older methods, while possibly somewhat restrictive in design, are known to perform well and assure reliable joints.

Glue

Glue joints depend upon two principal factors. First, proper mixing of the glue is absolutely essential in obtaining a good joint. Each glue manufacturer provides a recipe for the preparation of his product. The best way to insure good results is to follow the recipe faithfully, without the slightest deviation. Improper mixing can produce a weak resin, allow resin to escape from the joint, cause a short pot life, or any of several other serious deficiencies.

The second cardinal principle is that the correct pressure must be maintained on the joint while the glue cures. Too little pressure permits the parts to shift out of position, and frequently allows voids to form. Too much pressure can force glue out of the joint or even damage the parts. Either way, you're a loser because the joint is weak. Again, the manufacturer's instructions should be followed. A few observations are common to all glue joints, however. Obviously, the pressure must be adequate to hold the parts in position.

This doesn't take a great amount of force, but it does mean good firm holding. Softwoods might do well at about 100 psi, while the harder species take around 200 psi on the joint area.

Pressure can be applied best with clamps, and the best all-around type is the parallel-jaw woodworking type. Only wood or a softer material should bear against the work piece to spread the force. Nails, brads, wood screws, and bolts can provide glue joint pressure where clamping is not practical. Often, these elements can be removed after the glue cures. Where fabric goes over the surface later, as where wing skin is glued to ribs, any nails *must* be removed to prevent damage to the covering in service. Removal is facilitated by nailing through a thin strip of wood or a heavy cotton reinforcing tape.

Sometimes, where a part is so thin or small as to make nails and screws impractical, the parts can be made originally with excess material for nailing. The extra sections are cut off after the joint is made. In all cases, the size of nails or screws must be chosen carefully to avoid damage to the parts, and still provide ample glue pressure.

Parts to be joined by glue must be fitted together accurately enough to insure that the glue film does not exceed the manufacturer's recommended maximum thickness of about .030 in. Flat joints present no great problem in this respect. Contoured parts are quite difficult to cut accurately, so designers usually avoid joining two rigid contoured pieces. Instead, one member of the joint is made flexible enough to conform to the other at assembly, or it is steam-formed to fit before assembly.

Because the glue undergoes a complete change of physical state during cure, its properties change over a broad range between the time it is mixed and the final stage of cure. It can be spread easily during only a portion of this time. After one point in the cure, a satisfactory joint is impossible. The rate at which curing progresses is different when the glue is exposed to air than when the joint is closed. Before attempting to assemble a large unit, you must be familiar with the handling characteristics of your glue. It is necessary to plan your assembly work to be sure you have enough glue ready for all the work to be done at one time. The amount of work is limited by the length of time it takes to spread the glue on *both* surfaces of each joint, get the parts in position, and apply pressure. If you're slow and the glue gels before you close the joint or before you reach the final exact position for each piece, you'll probably have to make the detail parts over again.

Jigs

The largest assemblies definitely require some form of jig to hold parts in correct position for gluing. Before it gels, the average glue is surprisingly slippery, and even a heavy clamping pressure will not guarantee that large parts cannot move. Most of the major components of an airplane, such as a wing panel or fuselage section cannot be made completely self-jigging on assembly. Nails and brads can be used with caution. They should be used sparingly, and only in locations where the holes will not impair the strength of a part.

Self-jigging is one of the most valuable tricks available to the amateur builder. It can save many hours of work building even temporary holding fixtures for small assemblies. Naturally, the best place to incorporate this feature is right on the drawing board, but a lot can be done in the shop as the parts are made up. The idea is simple enough; just include a slot or groove here, and a shoulder there to provide a positive stop that locates a mating piece exactly in its correct position. The classic example of this is where a shaft fits into a hole. The hole fits tightly enough to locate the centerline, and a shoulder locates the end of the shaft. Some parts can be self-locating with excess material that is cut off after assembly. Simple as it is, this useful practice is overlooked by many designers.

Venting

Another thing frequently overlooked in wood assembly work is the crucially important drain hole, and its cousin—the vent. Wood is highly subject to decay through fungi and bacteria. These organisms thrive in warm, moist environments. That is precisely what you provide for them in a tightly closed wing assembly with a little condensed moisture in it. Under a July sun internal temperatures can reach 150°F. The wood itself, of course, is the food required by the growing organisms. The moisture can be reduced, if not entirely eliminated, by holes placed at *all* the low points where it might accumulate when the airplane is on the ground. That means every single bay in the wing, unless a fully connecting drainage path is provided.

Seaplanes cannot be treated exactly the same as a landplane, of course, for drain holes wouldn't be very practical in the bottom of a hull or float. The answer in their case is to provide access to all low pockets where water may collect, so that any accumulation can be removed by pumping or sponging. Protective treatments complete the job.

Adequate ventilation is nearly as important as drainage, because the film of moisture which doesn't drain can be just as damaging as the puddles. It is removed by adequate movement of fresh air through each compartment. In seaplanes, this is even more important than in land-based aircraft, as there is often some continuous seepage when the ship is afloat, in addition to occasional condensation.

Wood Preservatives

The service life of wood assemblies depends heavily upon the quality of surface protection given it. There are protective treatments on the market under various trade names which can give ample protection against the usual fungus and bacterial attacks. The growth-inhibiting chemicals can be incorporated into the finish materials, or can be applied separately. Manufacturer's instructions should be followed exactly for the particular material you choose. In any case, the final surface finish should generally follow the steps described below.

Sealer is the first component of any good finish system. This prevents excessive penetration of solvents into the wood, avoiding too rapid drying of the surface films. Solvents deeply penetrated into the wood evolve slowly, softening the finish materials applied over them. Commercial sealers are satisfactory, but it is necessary to make certain the one you choose is not affected by the solvents in your finish. You can mix your own, of spar varnish, with 12 ounces or more aluminum powder added per gallon. Two coats of spar varnish will be adequate for most interior surfaces, except floats and hull bottoms, which should have at least one additional aluminized coat or its equivalent. Where fabric and dope are to be used over the wood, a coat of dope-proof sealer or paint must be used.

If the wood surface is to carry the final finish directly, and a smooth exterior is desired, some filler will be necessary. The wood grain, and any depressions left from nailing, countersinking screws, or fabrication, must be filled up to the highest parts of the surface. Commercial fillers give satisfactory results, but again you must make sure the material is not damaged by the solvents in later coats. A filled surface must be sanded after each coat, to just barely expose the previous coat, until the low spots are filled right up flush. Putty of the same type as the filler should be used for any large depressions.

Generally, a finer grade of sandpaper is used with each successive coat of filler, starting with about number 100 grit garnet paper open-coated. The last coat should be finished with number 240 grit wet or dry. Wet sanding gives the smoothest finish much faster. The mud left from wet sanding can be removed quickly with damp sawdust, then traces of the sawdust can be brushed off with a dry cloth or soft brush.

Finishing

Doped fabric over wood requires one brush coat of clear dope, which is allowed to dry, followed by another brush coat. The fabric is laid into the wet second coat, and bubbles carefully worked out with a brush. After this dries, a brushed coat of clear dope is applied, followed by a minimum of one spray coat before the pigmented coats. The color coats are handled as for any fabric finish system. This is detailed in Chapter 4.

Finish applied directly on the wood, after the filler is completed, can be enamel, dope, or lacquer. Enamel is identical to spar varnish, except for the pigments added to it. Generally, at least one brushed coat of the final color is necessary to provide sufficient thickness for sanding and protection of the wood. When the wet-sanded color coats are smooth enough, a top coat can be sprayed on. This may require rubbing compound after it is thoroughly dry (several weeks minimum in warm weather) before a really high gloss is obtained. Contrary to some advertising claims, a genuine high quality finish is only possible with lots and lots of hand work, applied in many coats.

The most common pitfalls in finishing are insufficient drying between coats (all paints harden *slowly* and *shrink*), insufficient sanding, steel wool (it leaves broken fibers imbedded in the surface), and excessively rough abrasives. Probably next in importance is careless use of thinners. Particularly with the lacquers and dopes, this can lead to various faults such as failure to cover, or blushing and failure to harden. Whatever finish materials are being used it is especially important to follow the manufacturer's directions exactly for best results.

Repairs

Repairs to wood aircraft structures, as in the case of other materials, must conform to some approved design if the aircraft is to retain an airworthiness certificate. The first source for such a design is again Advisory Circular 43. 13-1. This document contains detailed descriptions of generally used acceptable repair procedures, and the limitations on safe use of these repairs. If the circular contains no suitable design for the particular case you have to repair, the airplane manufacturer's repair and maintenance manual should be checked.

Failing this, an inquiry to the manufacturer may turn up an approved repair design, especially if the damage is a common type. If no approved design can be found, then it is necessary to seek FAA approval of your own proposed repair. In no case should the repairs be made before engineering approval is obtained. When you submit a proposed repair design, you must also submit substantiating data to show that the repair will restore the original strength and function of the affected parts.

In general, the principles of repair are the same as those discussed in Chapter 2. The repair must either replace the original with something equally suitable, or restore exactly what was there before damage, wear and tear, or deterioration altered it.

Wood members can often be repaired by cutting out the affected material and gluing in a new piece of the same material, using an approved type scarf joint (refer to AC 43. 13-1). Another repair often used is gluing a patch over the affected area, with the edges of the patch bevelled sufficiently to avoid excessive stress concentration. In this case, the patch must supply enough structural strength to make up the original capacity of the member. Both solid and laminated or plywood members can be repaired by these methods.

After all glue joints have hardened, a repair should be refinished with the same materials as those used originally on the airplane.

9. Getting Everything Back Together

Now all the components are repaired and ready to be put together. Once again you'll have a whole, airworthy machine, a real honest-to-goodness flyin' machine. After those long weeks and months of work you may find it's hard to believe you've got this far. Well, you have—and with the best part to come, that first flight, so let's get crackin'. It's a good idea to arrange to have your mechanic get in with both feet at this point . . . he'll most likely want to, anyway . . . just so he'll know what he's signing his name to.

First, lay out all the hardware in logical sequence for the various components. Check to see that it's all there, airworthy and ready to be installed from arm's length. Second, set all the tools as and where they will be needed. Which part to install first depends on how the ship is constructed.

It's the usual practice to get the ship on its own feet first, so install the gear. If the gear's in the fuselage, you'll have to get that high enough to fit the gear in place—but only just high enough. Insert all bolts and nuts, and the shock system. If it's a tri-gear, then fit that and its mounting which may include the engine mount. Oh yes, a torque wrench should be used. Its values vary from 0, where castle nuts and cotter pins are used, to 300 inch-pounds for the hi-shear bolts that anchor Cessna's spring-steel gear and other rigid gear mountings. If it's supposed to move like the J-3 Cub, then make sure it does. If it's rigid then make sure it's installed as the manufacturer designed it to be. The service manual will give you detailed how-to-do-it instructions, so use it. If the gear is in the wings, then install the gear in the wings before you install the wings on the fuselage. Besides, with the wing upside down, it's easier to install the gear.

After the gear, the engine is next—if for no other reason than to balance the ship for easy handling.

Most tri-gear ships will not stay on three wheels but fall back on the tail skid. It doesn't make much difference with conventional gear. You will have a special problem though if you tie the ship out. It's several hundred pounds lighter so the wind can really play games. If you have to tie it out, then make sure the ropes and anchors will do the job. Set the tail up in level flight attitude and secure it there. The engine, as a rule, will have all the accessories installed: mags, starter, generator, harness, etc. You'll have to remember, or refer to your notes, as to what might interfere with the engine mount or nose wheel mount for your particular ship.

It helps to have the ship in level flight attitude especially if you are using friends to help lift the engine into position. If the mounts are vertical, as in most small ships, put the bolts (4) in the mount with the rubber shocks. The bolts should be in just enough to hold the shocks. Have the other parts close at hand.

Now pick up and position the engine to the mount; while it's being held in position all the other parts are installed and fastened at least finger-tight. Never let the engine hang by the top two bolts or you'll bend one of the members. The mount is designed to be two parts of the eternal triangle, the engine being the third part.

Once the mount bolts are tight and pinned, usually the baffle system is installed. It is very important that the baffles be installed just as approved in order that the engine cool properly. Much time and testing had to be done to see that the engine cooled to within limits for all conditions of flight. Then progressively . . . the exhausts with heater shrouds and all the air ducts to proper inlets and outlets should be installed and secured . . . carburetor and its controls. . . . throttle, mixture, heater hooked up and operation checked for proper travel. Also connect the gas line from the gascolator. With the mags installed and timed, the ground leads should be installed. Once all is secured and checked, the cowling can be left until after the engine has been run. There are usually adjustments to be made or "bugs" to be checked out, so leaving the cowling off will save the new paint. The prop will have to be installed, of course, but since it will have to be removed to install the cowling, just run a single piece of safety wire through all the bolts. Running the engine requires that the gas lines be secured for fuel to flow and this means installing the wings on most planes.

Since the wings are too large for one man to handle, you'll have to get everything ready. First, check all the hardware; lay it out where it's within easy reach of the point of installation. Tools for the most part will consist of a hammer and large drift pin. Check over the wing itself. Are all the fittings in place and tight? Gas gauge installed with its ground wire? Everything done which would be easier to do on the bench than after the wing is up on the fuselage? Although the wing will weigh more, the flaps and ailerons are more easily installed down low than up in position on the fuselage. This applies to the high-wing ship, of course; on low-wing planes it makes little difference.

Here's one additional point: if the gas connection is by hose fittings with clamps, position the hose as it would be with the wing on the plane, then tighten the one clamp on the wing side. Install the other clamp loosely but in a position which will be easy to get at with pliers and screwdriver. Then put a few drops of oil on the fuselage fittings. Don't forget to install a cord where it's needed to pull the cable through. Make sure the main wheels and tail wheel are checked.

With everything in readiness, lift the wing into position with the help of a few friends. If hose is used on the gas line, now is the time to slip it on. Then align the spar fittings; work them into alignment with the fuselage fittings. Sometimes it helps to put a drift pin in the first or easiest one that can be aligned. Then you can jack the other fitting into alignment, insert the bolt part way, then align the first fitting before tapping the bolt in all the way. Align the second fitting and insert the bolt. Make sure the man at the tip holds the wing in its correct position until at least the front strut has been installed. It's very important *not* to vary too much from this position at any time, since the wing butt fittings may be overstressed or even cracked. Line up the front strut and insert the bolt at the fuselage end first, then the wing fitting. Don't forget the tie-down rings if they're on the upper end of the strut.

At this point you'd check the dihedral if it's necessary. Most of the older strut-braced fabric ships have an adjustable rod at one end or the other of the front strut. The rear strut adjusts the wash-in or wash-out. Most manufacturers provide information on how to do this. Usually the ship is set up in level position both laterally and longitudinally. Then with a bubble protractor or a wire from tip to tip, the adjustment is made to the specs. It's trial-and-error till you've got it to the angle required. Wash-out is by reference to the inboard end of the wing as a base and the outboard end (usually at a point along the spar just before it tapers at the tip). The protractor is positioned between spars on the inboard end of the wing and set for zero; it is then moved to the outboard position and set for so many degrees, as required by the specs. You then adjust the rear strut until you get the bubble centered. Just remember wash-out is trailing edge of the wing up. On the other wing, it's the same . . . . UP. Once adjusted, secure all bolts with washers and nuts. Don't forget to tighten the jam nut on the rod end of the struts. You may have to adjust the rear strut a turn or two after you fly the ship, but at least the ship will be very near what the FAA originally had approved. For instance, wash-out affects the stall characteristics, dihedral the lateral stability and responsiveness of the ailerons. Wash-out can also affect the elevator trim, that is, the ship may trim nose-heavy with too much wash-out or tail-heavy with too little.

Before you put the nuts on the inboard fittings, check for gaps. Some fittings fit tightly, but others must have a washer or two slipped in between the fittings. In such cases, the fitting would be pre-stressed if you drew up on the nut. This could cause a fitting failure if high stresses were applied to the ship by strong gust loads or higher-than-normal speeds in gusty air. To insert a spacer washer use another bolt of the same diameter to back out the regular bolt. Insert the spacer or spacers and tap the bolt back in. Secure with a nut. Avoid turning the bolt in the fitting if possible, as steel fittings might score the bolt's shank. Once you've tightened all the bolts, tighten the gas lines and pair off the electrical connections to each wing and check them all out for correct operation.

Next install the ailerons and flaps. This is usually a two-man operation but one man *can* do it—if he's careful. Better lubricate all bearings and bolts at this point. Use an undersize pin in one of the hinge points; then insert the other regular bolt. Next take out the pin and install regular bolts. As a general rule, all bolts are installed pointing inboard. When all bolts or pins are inserted, secure them with washers and nuts or cotter pins. Some installations should be brought up tight, others only finger-tight. The main idea is to make sure they are all secured. If you have previously installed cord to the control cables now's the time to use it. Tie a loose knot, then have someone with a rag hold the cable in tension as you put the cord and cable through. If it gets caught on a rib you will have to pull back and forth gently to get the knot through the rib. One purpose of the cord is to keep the cables from getting crossed as they're pulled through. If there was no cord you'll just have to fish the cables through the inspection hole in each rib by reaching through the inspection holes. Check carefully to see that you've got the right hole. Use a mirror or listen for the binding of the cable over the edge of the hole. Once all the cables have been threaded, install the pulleys as necessary to complete the linkage.

After you've checked again for crossed and misaligned cables and set them properly, install the bolts and/or turnbuckles either to the idlers or the aileron horns, whichever is the case. If no turnbuckles have been broken then you'll have to muscle the last bolt into position. If you've broken a turnbuckle, then turn up until you've got a little tension on the aileron controls.

Now link up the aileron control arms and secure them. Usually the flaps aren't as complicated but get them hooked up now so you can adjust the four surfaces in alignment. Start with the ailerons. Center the control wheel or stick and block it into position rigidly. Check the chain or cables at the yoke for center or equal length on either side of the wheel sprocket in most controlwheel installations. Trace the cable on back through to the ailer-

Tail surfaces being installed shortly before towing the fuselage to the airport.

ons. If all are in position at all pulleys, then start to adjust the turnbuckles to bring the aileron idlers into their centered position. If no idlers are installed, then you'll move the ailerons into a centered position as you go along. With idlers, you'll adjust the aileron control arms to bring the ailerons into proper alignment. Cable tension should be about 20 to 40 pounds; the manual will give you the limits. Install the aileron stops and check for proper control limits; adjust to specs. The flap cables are usually only one for each with a spring for the top side. The cable for each flap usually ties into a single cable, then onto the pilot's control handle. Stinson 108 models have a particular quirk in that the cable can get caught under a chafing block so that it rubs on the elevator torque tube. In time it can saw a slot in the tube and weaken it. It's under the floor boards and hard to see, so can be missed. Usually the flap cables are adjusted so that each flap will start down at the same time with just a smidgin of play at the handle. Once you have adjusted the aileron and flap systems and have checked for smooth operation without undue friction or binding . . . *safety the turnbuckles!*

All that needs to be done now are electrical connections and the gas lines. Check out the lights and gas gauges, if electric, and then put some gas in the tanks—enough to check for leaks and fuel-flow through all strainers. Make sure it's gas you're getting—not water! Run off enough for the check, at least a quart from each tank at the firewall gascolator. Before you install the wing

Threading the trim tab cables can be perplexing at times.

roof and strut fairings, get someone else (usually your mechanic) to look over everything in that area. Then fit and secure the fairing around the wings. Let the strut fairing go until you've flown and adjusted the rigging if necessary.

Of the major components to be replaced, this leaves the tail feathers. Start by laying out the surfaces and all the hardware in the proper location and within easy reach. Don't forget tools and the oil or grease can. Now stop a minute and check your notes or the service manual. If you don't have either, make a dry run. What's the sequence of assembly? If the whole tail has been removed, you'll find the stabilizer is first, then the elevators, fin and rudder (on most fabric-covered ships, the fin is part of the fuselage). With a knife, carefully cut away any fabric which might interfere with the installation (on a fabric-covered fuselage, that is). Also remove paint which will make pins and bolts a problem to install and will make the controls stiff. Thread the cables and trim wires for easy access after assembly of the various surfaces. Most metal surfaces line up well so it's a matter of working with the bolts until you can get them lined up and in place. Tubular steel, fabric-covered surfaces usually take a bit of pushing and banging to get the tubing and respective bolt holes lined up. A little grease on the tubes helps; a tapered awl will also help in the final line-up. Insert all bolts down and inboard unless this wasn't the way they were originally installed by the manufacturer. Once the stabilizer is in place and secured, install first the one and then the other elevator. Just slip the bolts on the hinges, then connect the arm between the two. Now thread the cables, link to the elevator and check for direction and freedom of movement. If all is well, install all the washers and nuts. You'll find there's a rule that's mighty important: *Never install a bolt without securing it properly before you leave it!* Break this rule and it may break *you*—for all time. If you are installing a series of pins or bolts, then secure them as a series, but *never* leave even one, until all nuts are tightened and cotter pins are installed.

Cotter pins must be spread and nuts run up with at least 1½ threads showing. Where a castle nut is used it must have a cotter pin installed. Elastic or lock type nuts can be installed even on bolts with a cotter pin hole. Bolts should be long enough so that no threads are in bearing, yet the nut should not bottom on the unthreaded shank. Use washers to get the correct spacing, but don't carry this too far . . . two or three washers would be the limit. Instead get the next size shorter bolt. They're cheap so you might as well do it right.

With the horizontal surfaces secured and functioning, install the fin and rudder in the same manner. Don't forget to check the control travel for proper limits before you get too far. Many of the fabric ships have tail brace wires. Usually they'll have to be adjusted for proper alignment. Do this while you have the ship set up in level attitude for the wing rigging check. Adjust the wires to get them level and vertical, then tighten to a low twang. Secure the jam nuts all around. Oh, don't forget the tail light and beacon, if installed on the tail. Also the Omni antenna. Now you are just about ready for the finishing touches: fairing, cowling, prop.

10. Finally . . . Let's Fly

Now's the time, with all the major components assembled, to begin the check-out of all the systems, to make necessary adjustments, to run the preflight, to test ground handling and finally . . . finally . . . to experience that moment that is like no other you've ever known . . . that moment you're flyin' in a ship you've put together with your own hands!

Although the fittings aren't a system let's go over them again. Check all bolts, pins, clevis bolts, for tightness and security. Walk around the ship with a hand full of wrenches. Check the security of each fastener. You'll have to be your own inspector at this point. If you find one that's not the way you feel it should be, then rework it right then and there. The very fact that you are looking for anything that's not right, after it's *supposed* to be right, will help you to find it.

After the fittings, go on to the control system: ailerons, elevator, rudder, flaps, trim tabs, brakes, gear retraction. Check for smoothness and limits of operation. Does one interfere with the other? Are they too loose or too tight? Use a mirror and a light to look and watch as the controls and cables move from one extreme to the other. Two cables may be wrapped around each other or through the wrong lightening hole and you'd never feel it. Is every pulley and fair lead safetied so the cable can't jump the pulley? Sometimes the smallest detail can give you the biggest heart flutter . . . after you're up and away.

It may sound silly, but check as you go over the ship for loose miscellaneous items or tools (even boards) you might have left in the back of the fuselage when you had to crawl back there. Don't laugh, it *has* happened! You could find bucking bars, tools, anything in some unlikely place. Loose change which fell out of your pocket or hardware you'd dropped . . . it could become wedged in the most unlikely place and jam a control.

Does the airspeed work? Check the pitot and static systems. If the lines are crossed the airspeed will work backwards. A simple test is to blow gently into the pitot tube (just a puff) and have someone see if the airspeed works in the right direction. If so, then blow enough to get cruising speed for the aircraft . . . then use your tongue to plug the end. If it doesn't work then you'll have to hunt for the leak. Maybe there's a break in the line (fast bleed-off) or a loose hose or pipe fitting (usually a slow bleed-off). Of course it can be the instrument itself. Unhook the connecting line and blow through one end while the other end is plugged . . . if it's tight then it may be the instrument. Also check the location of the head of the pitot and the position of the static openings. If not in the approved positions you might get a very different reading from what you should.

If you've had the brakes apart or have uncoupled a brake line, it's got air in the lines. Even a single bubble will affect the operation quite noticeably. A pressure bleeder will make the job easy but you can do just as well by hand, only it takes longer and needs an extra pair of hands. Fill the reservoir, using the right type of hydraulic fluid of course, then pump the brake till you feel some pressure build up. If you can't get any pressure, then check master and wheel cylinders for leakage or defective "O" rings. When you do get pressure have a friend open the bleed screw at the wheel cylinder as you work the deal from full up to full down; then close the screw. Repeat this operation until you get the air out of the system and you'll have a high, hard pedal. If both wheels are on one master cylinder, bleed one wheel until all the air is out, then do the same for the other. At this point you should get a hard pedal or handle and have effective brakes.

While you're there check the wheels. Is the cotter pin in place? Does the wheel spin free, yet have no side play? The conventional gear usually has a steerable tail wheel linked either to the rudder or the rudder cables. With the rudder centered, adjust the spring's chain linkage to give enough tension to keep the steering cam engaged, yet able to swivel full when you need to. It may take a few trials in different positions and even taxiing the ship around to get the right adjustment.

The tri-cycle gear usually has a rod linkage directly to the rudder pedals. So adjust the rod ends to center both the rudder pedals and the nose wheel, then hold this position and center the rudder by adjusting the rudder cables. At this point check the rudder and nose wheel stops; they should both touch at the same time. Also, how about the shimmy damper? Does it offer resistance? It should, otherwise you'll shake hell out of things if the nose wheel is even a little out of balance.

Better give a final look under the panel. Are the controls free? Any loose wires, hoses? . . . Tape them out of the way. Fuel or primer lines should not have any wiring taped to them. All instruments and radios tight and supported? Rough air or a rough landing can reposition them with possible restriction of the movement of the control yoke, causing acute discomfort . . . possibly of a permanent nature.

This leaves only the engine to check out but so far we haven't put gas on board. Put about five gallons in one tank then check for leaks at all connections. No leaks? Good! Now position the tank selector for that tank and drain out a half gallon through the firewall gascolator. This may give you a start if no gas flows. It wouldn't be the first time a selector handle was installed in the wrong position. Correct it, fill that tank, then do the same for the other tank or tanks. Check each for proper operation and flow. You can drain a gallon from each tank using all quick drains and gascolators. If you use a glass bottle you'll be able to see water or other contamination. Don't forget to fill the tanks and check the gauges for correct indications.

Now check over everything forward of firewall. See that all the controls are secured and functioning, all plugs tight and ignition leads traced through to the proper plugs. Are the "P" leads (shielded wires to the ignition switch) installed from the mags to the ignition switch? Make sure that the baffles are in place, all hoses clamped tight, primer lines hooked up and supported, generator and starter cables connected. See that the carburetor heater control works the valve freely and fully. You'll lose some power if the heat is partly on and may not get enough heat when you need it.

Oil . . . is it in the engine? It's a good idea to hang a tag on the throttle or ignition switch such as "No Oil" just as a reminder.

Up to this point we may not have had our mechanic friend in attendance but now we need him. He's going to have to check over the whole ship before you put the inspection plates and fairing on anyway, so call him. He might find what you didn't notice or just plain missed because you've been so close to the machine for so long.

Once he's given his okay, you may as well run the engine while he's looking on . . . just in case you have a problem or two. First, though, get the chocks under both wheels and tie down the tail . . . this one we don't want to get away . . . yet. Okay . . . gas on . . . a little prime . . . crack the throttle . . . mixture rich . . . flip over a couple of times . . . now the switch . . . and give it a whirl.

Once started, check the oil pressure immediately. Don't take your eyes off the instrument till it comes up to normal. If you don't get pressure within 60 seconds, shut it down and find out *why*. Then with the oil pressure normal we can go on with the warm-up . . . check the mags, (left, right and off) carburetor, heat, prop, generator then back to idle. Idle is around 450 to 600 on the average engine, but your manual will give the correct range. Run the engine through from idle to full throttle at various speeds of throttle application. The acceleration should be smooth and without pause or backfire. Also run the engine at full throttle for at least two minutes. This will check fuel flow. You might do this with the tail down to simulate a climb condition. Any loss of power should be checked for cause before flight.

Also what static RPM do you get? Is it too high or too low? It could be the prop's not pitched right. What about vibration? If things are jumping on the panel, you may have an unbalanced prop or it's out of track. The track is easy to check even while running. Let the engine idle, then stand off to the side, looking in line with the prop arc against a contrasting background. If you see both blades instead of one then shut her down and check for how much . . . 1/8"at the tips is maximum.

To check the track, set the prop vertical, then place the edge of a can up to it, but not touching, at the tip. Now turn the prop (check for switch off) backwards or clockwise till the other blade reaches your reference point. Note the distance, then bring the original blade around again to see that your reference hasn't moved . . . up to $\frac{1}{8}''$ is okay. If it's more, check a few inches up the blade; if it's still off, better have the prop checked by a prop shop.

Any oil leaks or anything loose? Are oil pressure and temperature in normal range? If your mechanic is satisfied then you're ready for the cowling, prop and spinner. If you have to remove the prop to put the cowling on then you'll have to retorque the prop bolts and safety them again. Remember to choke up on the wrench when tightening the prop bolts. A firm pull at $6''$ is all that's needed. Too much torque is almost as bad as too little. There will be some form of locking—either stop nuts or safety wire.

Sometimes the cowling must be installed before the prop, but whatever the sequence, now is the time. Cowlings can be cantankerous. You'll just have to fool around with it until it fits properly. Remember to check the prop and spinner for clearance (also for inside, on Lycoming engines). The starter plate will grind a ridge real quick. Check also the fittings of the baffle system to insure proper cooling. Sometimes the cowling latches must be adjusted to complete the final fitting.

With all in readiness this is no time to regress—but how about your paper work? Logs signed? Weight and balance computed? Registration applied for? Radio license application filed? If it's a home-built contact the FAA agent to see if he wishes to be present for the first flight or at least get his final okay.

You're eager to get in the air but let's consider the weather. Pick a calm early morning with little or no traffic at your field. If there is a wind it should be light and right down the best and longest runway with at least one good field up-wind just in case.

Now start as if you were flying any other ship . . . with a pre-flight. Walk around, looking over the ship; then check the *gas* and *oil,* quantity as well as octane. Check all drains for good flow. Get in and buckle up. Have a plan of action, a flight plan. Just what are you going to do if this or that happens? Think it out so you'll have a course of action ready.

With Type-Certificated aircraft you'll know the stalling speed, take-off distance, climbing speed and rate of climb. With the home-built this information may be a bit vague. So you'll have to get some of this information bit by bit.

Let's assume you've made the before take-off check and you're all ready to go. Today even the small airports have 2500- to 3000-foot runways or better, so try a fast taxi and feel how the ship reacts. But remember to set a limit say ⅔ or ¾ of the distance down the runway—where you're going to cut the power and roll to a stop without leaving the airport. It would even be a good idea to place a red flag at this point so you can see it from the left side. As you increase your taxi speeds you'll notice that first the rudder, then the elevator, and finally the ailerons become effective to some extent. You can get some idea of their responsiveness as the speed is increased up to, but not over, the stall speed.

If runway length permits, you can proceed into a slow flight condition a few feet off the runway. Start with full power to accelerate rapidly; then as you feel the ship wants to fly, reduce the power so as to maintain the low speed. One point to keep in mind: You've got to have a point on the runway (say halfway) past which you'll cut power, land the ship and stop. As you gain experience and feel of the ship you'll be able to judge how far to go and still stop safely. You'll be able then to extend your flight duration from a few seconds to as much as 30 or 45 seconds. You'll be able also to determine the stall speed, responsiveness of the controls, the rigging and, from position of the controls, the balance and stability of the ship. You'll be able to stop and make adjustments without ever leaving the airport. Two things you should keep in mind at all times: Set up a point at which you will cut the power and have plenty of room to land and stop; and never take your eyes off the runway ahead or allow the nose to obscure the runway. It's a personal discipline you'll have to hold to without deviation.

Once you're satisfied that the ship flies with enough control and performance for safe flight, then, and only then will you *plan* to leave the confines of the runway and commit yourself to the freedom of flight. Before you do this, though, you should return to the line and give the ship another preflight. Look the whole craft over. Has anything vibrated loose? Any oil leaks? How about the gas and oil . . . got enough? If something needs adjusting get it done now.

Then and only then start up. Taxi to the longest runway with the least obstructions and the field's best up-wind. Run the before-take-off check, clear traffic, take all the runway you can get, line up and give it full power. Let it roll till it feels light, then ease off slowly, leveling off at a few feet and allowing the speed to pick up. At this point you can still cut the power and land . . . beyond it, you're committed.

Let the speed pick up to about 50% above your stalling speed and use this as your climbing speed. If the stall is 50 mph then climb at 75 mph. Once you reach this speed climb straight out without any turns till you get some altitude, say 1000 to 1500! . . . then you can make a gentle turn to circle the field. For the time being limit the speed to 25% above stall speed and trim to maintain this speed in level flight.

Now you'll have time to think a bit about other things, check over the instruments . . . oil pressure, oil temperature, airspeed. . . . look around constantly for traffic and keep track of where you are. Usually you should be out in the wide open spaces, not over congested areas.

Let's see how the ship flies hands-off. If you've done a job with the rigging on the ground you shouldn't be very far out. So what pressures do you have to hold for level flight at cruising? Try releasing the controls. . . . how does the ship react? If the wing drops before the nose starts to turn you'll need to adjust a wing strut to wash-in or out the wing. If the nose turns before the wing drops then you'll have to adjust the rudder trim. It's a trial-and-error method until you get the ship to fly hands-off. Sometimes the flaps may need adjustment and they will act like the ailerons but not as effectively, being closer to the center of gravity. To get a fine trim you'll need smooth air, such as you'd get early in the morning or late in the afternoon just before dark. Then you'll have to look for tendencies to drift one way or another and of course make minute corrections.

You'll want to make a check of control stability on amateur-built ships that isn't necessary for production or TC'd types. It's to see that the controls will react in a passive manner during all conditions of flight from slow all the way to the highest speed you may wish to fly the ship.

First you've got to be sure that the controls are balanced with counterweights as called for in the construction drawings. This would apply to the production types as well. These counterweights must be installed and secured. Most service manuals give you information on how to check for proper balance of the control surfaces. At any rate don't get the ship (home-built) much over the climbing speed till you check the controls in the following manner.

Take each control in turn and knock it sharply to get at least a 3° deflection, then observe how it returns to neutral. Does it do so without any oscillation? It should. Try this three or four times with each control, then increase the speed about five mph each time and check the controls again, all three, at this speed. If at any time the control passes neutral before stopping, don't try any higher speed but land and check the control systems for balance, looseness of cables and hinges. If you can't find anything wrong get some professional help. The FAA or a DER.

The other tests for stability are longitudinal (rudder) and lateral (elevators). For longitudinal you kick the rudder and release it. Does it produce an ever-decreasing oscillation? If so, this is static stability. If the nose keeps yawing the same amount each time then it's neutral; but if the yaw keeps increasing . . . . . something ain't right and you'll have to find out why. It might be that you forgot to install the fin or rudder???

The elevators are usually more critical because the balance relationship between the center of gravity for the ship and the center of lift can change depending on how you load the ship. This is why you have C.G. range limits for all aircraft and why it's important to know how the ship is loaded. Chapter 1 covered the weight and balance problem. The elevators should have static stability but many just barely make the grade. If you get the balance too far aft or forward you'll be constantly working the elevators. That can be quite tiring after a few hours . . . . What's worse, dangerous.

Don't confuse stability and flutter. The first is how the aircraft reacts, and the second is how the control surface reacts, to flight conditions.

Well, you're on your own now. If you'll give your proud lady the respect and care she deserves you'll find she'll give you many hours of carefree enjoyment.

B
BEND ANGLE
R'
A
SETBACK
B
FLAT PATTERN LENGTH

1. R = INSIDE BEND RADIUS PLUS HALF OF THICKNESS.
2. PLACE STRAIGHTEDGE THRU R AND BEND ANGLE.
3. READ SETBACK ALLOWANCE ON CENTER SCALE

1.20
1.0
.8
.6
.4
R
(INCHES)
.2
.1
.08
.06
.04
.03

10.0
1.0
SETBACK
.10
(INCHES)
.01
.001
.0001

160
140
120
100
90
80
BEND
ANGLE
70
(DEGREES)
60
50
40
30
20

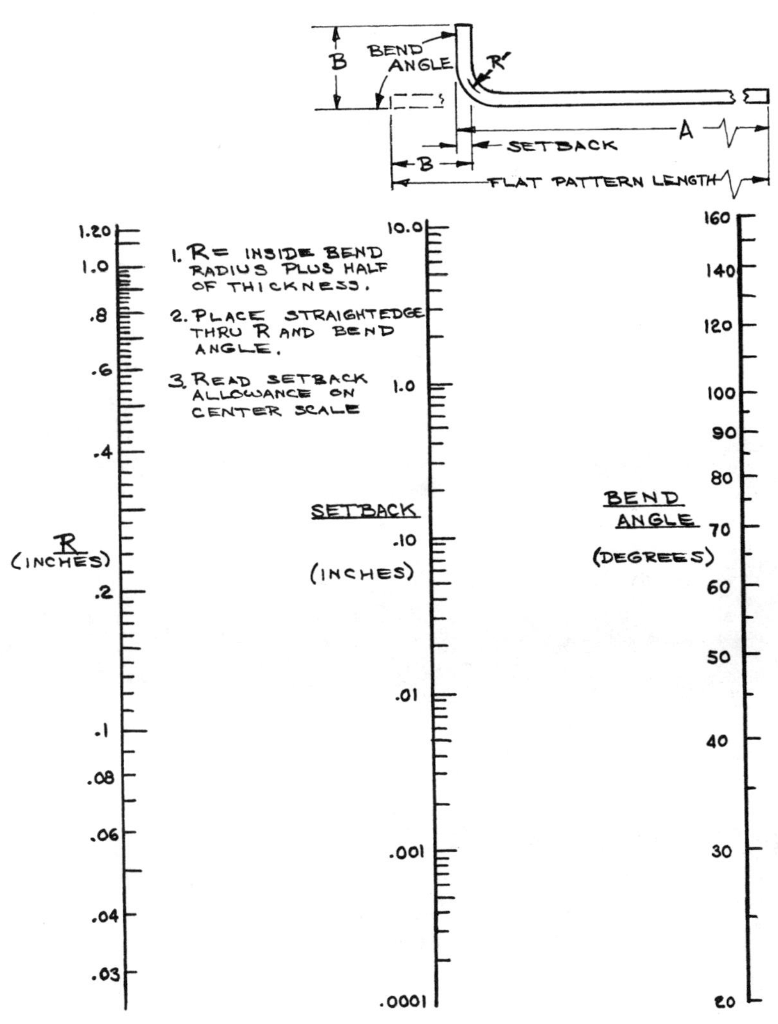

SETBACK